Robb

Robber Hopsika wasn't an ordinary highwayman. He never said, 'Your money or your life,' because he didn't want lives, and in any case to address strangers in such a manner would not have been polite. So he took their money with a bow, kissed the ladies' hands and departed with many thank yous. But when a rich gentleman offers him the chance of great wealth if he steals not something but someone, and when that someone turns out to be his lovely daughter Josephine who is held in the clutches of the notorious rogue Master Irongrip, Hopsika gallops into action with new vigour. His colourful misadventures make a fine, rip-roaring tale.

'Fantasy and familiarity are cleverly blended in an entertaining, fast-moving tale.' Junior Education

Also available in Lions

MR POPPER'S PENGUINS Richard & Florence Atwater
JEMIMA AND THE WELSH RABBIT Gillian Avery
THE SEARCH FOR DELICIOUS Natalie Babbitt
SIMON AND THE WITCH Margaret Stuart Barry
THE KING OF THE COPPER MOUNTAINS Paul Biegel
A BEAR CALLED PADDINGTON Michael Bond
HARRIET THE SPY Louise Fitzhugh
MY FATHER'S DRAGON Ruth Stiles Gannett
PRIVATE, KEEP OUT! Gwen Grant
THE DEMON BIKE RIDER Robert Leeson
THE LION BOOK OF HUMOROUS VERSE Ruth Petrie
MIND YOUR OWN BUSINESS Michael Rosen
THE RESCUERS Margery Sharp
DOMINIC William Steig
MARY POPPINS P. L. Travers
RABBITING ON Kit Wright

PAUL BIEGEL

Robber Hopsika

Translated by Patricia Crampton

Illustrated by Jan Brychta

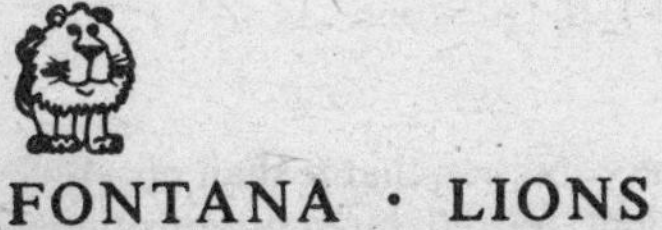

First published 1977 in Holland
First published 1978 in Great Britain by J. M. Dent & Sons Ltd
First published in Fontana Lions 1980
by William Collins Sons & Co Ltd
14 St James's Place, London SW1

Printed in Great Britain
by William Collins Sons & Co Ltd, Glasgow

Contents

Contents

1 The Robber Hopsika

The robber Hopsika no longer had a mother. Sometimes he had to have a good cry about it—as a robber—for when his mother was still alive he had been a good little boy. A very good little boy, in nicely polished shoes and white socks with never a mark on them.

But on the day his mother died Hopsika suddenly became a robber. He bought a horse and boots with silver spurs and galloped up the road, singing loudly, afraid of nothing and no one. 'I'm a robber!' he cried, and doffed his hat politely to everyone he met—unless it happened to be a coachload of rich people. Then Hopsika would fling his lasso over the coachman's head, drag him off his box into the sand, leap at full gallop from his own horse to the leading horse of the team and take them all to a quiet spot. There he would stop, open the door of the coach, remove his hat politely and say: 'Good morning, ladies and gentlemen, your money, please!'

He never said: *'Your money or your life!'* because Hopsika did not want lives and in any case, to address strangers in such a manner would not have been polite.

Generally the rich passengers were so terrified

that they handed over their full purses to Hopsika at once, but sometimes one of the gentlemen would try to be daring and show fight. This always made the robber Hopsika laugh. 'Whoops!' he would cry and, with a lightning movement, he would have the gentleman hanging high on a tree. If his hat fell off as he went, Hopsika would pick the hat up and throw it deftly up onto the gentleman's head among the branches. 'Keep it on, my dear sir,' he would cry. 'You really don't have to be that polite.'

He always took the money bags with a courteous bow. 'Thank you very much, thank you, thank you,' his robber's voice would repeat, as if he were collecting for a good cause.

Sometimes Hopsika threw the bags playfully into the air, juggling with two or three at once, and catching them with a clink. 'Sounds to me like a goodly sum,' he would remark and then he would kiss the ladies' hands. They would blush fiery red, or collapse in a swoon.

'I'm not going to bite your fingers off, you know,' cried Hopsika, picking up a lady in this state. 'All I want is your gold ring,' he added comfortingly. 'You can resume your journey at once. You have your whole life ahead of you, haven't you?'

He would even take the trouble to turn the coach round, which always meant a great to-do with all the horses, but when the coachman finally came stumbling up, having followed the tracks after his fall from the box, the coach was ready to travel on.

By then Hopsika had disappeared at a gallop, on the way to his secret house, where he lived very much alone, and burst into tears in front of his mother's portrait.

'Oh Mother, oh Mother, I have done it again, I've been bad again, look how much!' And under the eyes of the portrait, he shook out the money bags and counted out the golden florins and silver ducats. 'A hundred and twenty-three!' he sobbed. 'How awful, how awful, I'll take them back at once.'

But on the way Hopsika had to buy this and that: something good to eat and something pretty for his lonely house, and he gave the rest of the money to beggars and other unfortunates in the village. Every day was the same. He rode out singing, galloped along the road, doffed his hat politely to everyone and held up the rich coaches.

But on one occasion, when he had done it again and was busy turning the coach and six horses round so that the robbed passengers could continue their journey with the lives which were still their own, one of the robbed gentlemen called out: 'Hey you, will you listen to me?'

Hopsika turned: 'I don't think you really meant that "Hey you".'

'Sir,' said the gentleman, 'would you like to earn a great deal of money?'

'Earn?' said Hopsika. 'Stealing is more fun. I mean . . . Oh, Mother, Mother!' He began to sob.

Nonplussed, the gentleman went on: 'You could earn something by stealing something.'

The robber Hopsika dried his tears at once.

'How's that?' he asked.

The gentleman took Hopsika on one side. 'Listen,' he said, 'you are a very skilful robber. For me you must steal not *something*, but *someone*.'

'What's that you say?' asked Hopsika.

The gentleman brushed away a tear. 'My daughter,' he said, 'my lovely daughter Josephine ran away and fell into the hands of a rogue who makes her do the dirty work in his household.' A second tear welled up in the gentleman's eye.

'The rascal!' cried Hopsika. He too began to cry. 'Tell me where she lives and I will steal your daughter back.'

'Thank you,' said the gentleman. 'The rogue lives in the impregnable fortress of Irongrip. If you

bring her back you will earn a thousand golden florins.'

'Done,' said Hopsika, and doffing his hat he galloped back to his lonely house.

'Mother, I'm going to turn honest!' he told the portrait.

But the eyes stared back at him as if they were afraid, afraid of that one word, Irongrip.

2 The Fortress of Irongrip

'Don't be frightened, Mother!' cried the robber Hopsika. He spread five sandwiches with cheese and one with jam, polished his boots and their silver spurs until they shone, took the portrait down from the wall and said: 'Come with me, then you can see how I do it.' With the portrait under his arm he galloped up the road, singing loudly and doffing his hat to everyone he met.

'Wait a bit,' he muttered after a time. 'Am I going the right way?' For the fortress of Irongrip might lie north or east, south or west.

He asked a farmer, but he didn't know.

He asked a woman, but she didn't know either.

He asked a gentleman, but he ran away.

'And here comes a trump,' thought Hopsika, as he saw in the distance something shaped not unlike the ace of spades, a high, black coach.

'Pay attention, Mother,' said Hopsika. He hung the portrait on a branch and, as the coach passed him, he flung his lasso over the coachman's head, dragged him off the box into the sand, jumped onto the lead horse of the team, brought them to a halt, opened the door and said: 'Ladies and gentlemen . . .'

The rich travellers were already producing their money bags: they recognized Hopsika. But the robber said: 'No, no. No money today. I want to know the way, the way to the fortress of Irongrip.'

To Hopsika's amazement all the ladies swooned and the gentlemen turned pale as death.

'Don't go there,' said one.

'It means death,' said another.

And the third offered Hopsika his money bag. 'Take it and promise me never to set foot in that place.'

The robber began to laugh, white teeth flashing. 'I didn't ask for that,' he roared. 'I asked the way.' But the gentleman was silent and the ladies still in a swoon. Hopsika shut the door and turned away. There was the coachman, stumbling up.

'Ah!' cried the robber, 'you're the one I want.'

'No, no,' begged the coachman, falling to his knees.

'I only want to know where Irongrip is—that fine fortress,' said Hopsika.

The coachman jumped to his feet. 'I can tell you *that*,' he cried, beaming. 'Thirteenth on the left and then thirteenth on the right and at the end you'll see it, straight ahead of you.'

'Thanks, my good man,' said Hopsika. 'Have a

nice journey!' and he took off his hat politely as the coach started up.

'We got rid of him all right,' laughed the coachman. 'Just let him go there—to that "fine fortress". Fair enough!' His laugh was grim. He had a nasty bruise from his fall off the box into the sand.

But Hopsika laughed happily. 'You see, Mother, that's the way it goes,' he cried, 'and no robbery!' With the portrait under his arm he galloped on along the road, counting the turnings up to thirteen. This was a narrow, muddy path and his horse whinnied as he turned along it. It walked sluggishly, more and more sluggishly, its hooves going clomp-clomp in the muck.

The thirteenth turning to the right climbed steeply uphill and Hopsika's horse did not want to take it.

'Forward, old boy,' said the robber, 'don't be so lazy.' He stroked his horse's flanks with the silver spurs and the horse took the hill at full gallop. The spurs were razor-sharp. The road had thirteen bends and past the thirteenth bend lay the fortress of Irongrip, high up on a cliff. It was a strange building, with towers and walls and very small windows, but the strangest thing of all was the iron railing running along the top of the wall, points curving out, like iron claws held high, ready to pounce with their sharp tips.

'Most inviting,' murmured Hopsika. He reined in his horse and surveyed the fortress at his leisure. 'A clever notion, Mother, don't you think?' and he held up the portrait so that the eyes could see the fortress; it looked almost as if the frame began to quiver. 'As soon as anyone tries to climb the wall,' he said, 'the claws snap down behind him and he's trapped. Neat idea.'

Hopsika plucked a blade of grass, chewed it and spat it out again. Then he began on his sandwiches—the cheese ones and the one with jam. 'We're supposed to get the lovely Josephine out of there,' he said, with his mouth full. 'Oh, I beg your pardon, Mother, that was very rude of me,' and he hastily swallowed the mouthful. Later Hopsika turned his horse and galloped down the steep path again, all round the thirteen bends, and knocked at a farmhouse door at the bottom.

'Good morning,' he said, doffing his hat politely to the farmer's wife. 'Could I sleep here tonight and buy a scarecrow from you?'

'Have you any money?' asked the farmer's wife.

Hopsika jumped. 'Money,' he said, 'I never thought of that. Wait, I'll go and get some along the road. Keep this safe for me.' He thrust the portrait of his mother into her hands. 'I'll be back in a trice!'

3 A Meeting

Clomp-clomp went Hopsika and his horse down the muddy path towards the road to rob some money for a night's sleep and a scarecrow.

But even before he had reached the road, he met someone coming towards him, also mounted. It began with a ghastly whinny from both animals, as if they had taken a dislike to each other, even at a distance.

'What terrible horse language!' muttered Hopsika. 'The rider won't have any manners himself either, of course; but he may have money.'

'Hey there!' he cried. 'Is that how you bring up your beast? That's no language for a horse.'

The rider stopped. He was wearing a wide black cloak and a hat pulled down to his eyes, and he uttered a single word: 'Off!'

Hopsika stopped too, in the middle of the path, 'Off, *sir*, I expect you mean?' he asked pleasantly, and removed his hat.

For answer the other began to undo his cloak slowly, so that the belt beneath it was uncovered. Thirteen daggers glittered there—razor-sharp.

'Ah!' cried Hopsika in surprise, 'you're a knife-grinder, are you? Pity I haven't got my sandwich knife with me.'

The rider was unmoved. He simply pushed back his cloak a little further and a second belt came into view. In it were thirteen pistols, triggers already cocked.

'Ah!' cried Hopsika still more cheerfully, 'now I get it: you collect old bits and pieces!'

'Off!' hissed the rider.

'After you,' Hopsika replied, with a courteous bow.

'I'll count up to one,' shouted the rider, his hand straying towards the belts. But before he could count one, Hopsika had put spurs to his horse. Not the galloping spurs, the bucking spurs. *Whoops* went his horse's hind legs, and *whoops* flew Hopsika through the air, to land opposite the other rider, on his saddle. Robber and rider, face to face.

'Hm,' said Hopsika, feeling the daggers with his thumb, 'these could be a bit sharper. Could I just try out one of the pistols?' He already had two in his hands and fired them off, *pang pang,* into the air. 'Sounds just a mite rough—and this one is a bit crooked,' he said critically. 'Hardly worth a florin.'

He pushed them back into the belt and suddenly felt the rider's hands in an iron grip round his throat, turning it slowly, in order to break his neck.

Hopsika let him go on. 'I feel,' he thought, 'as if the world were turning round me while I keep still.' But when he could almost see his own back he gave a little flick with his silver spurs against the horse's fore-legs. It reared, with a whinny not meant for other horses' ears, robber and rider fell off—that is: Hopsika shot downwards and the rider upwards, up a tree.

'Sir!' cried Hopsika, 'I'm not just a Christmas goose waiting to have its neck wrung. In any case, that's for December and it's only March now.'

A pistol shot was the answer and the bullet struck the sand close to Hopsika.

'The barrel's crooked, just as I said,' cried the robber. 'You'll have to aim better.' So saying, Hopsika jumped onto his own horse and clomped away down the muddy path. But ten metres on he stopped, staring at an object he was holding in his hand.

'Hey,' he cried, looking over his shoulder, 'hey, you up there in the branches, I've just realized: you're Irongrip from the fort! Himself, so to speak. I can see it from your purse.'

A furious roar was his answer.

'Not exactly a nightingale,' murmured Hopsika. He lifted his voice to the branches again. 'That's because,' he called, 'when we were having that little turn there, I had a delightful opportunity to take some of your money.' He opened the purse in his hand. 'Just enough!' he called. 'Thank you very much. See you tomorrow, for I plan to pay you a visit. About eleven o'clock, will that do? Strong coffee, preferably, with plenty of sugar. Get Josephine to set the tray and bring it in.'

Ouch, perhaps it hadn't been very sensible to say that last bit, thought Hopsika, while his horse clomped on towards the farm where he was to spend the night. Irongrip would be sure to realize that he wanted to steal the lovely Josephine. Oh well, thought Hopsika, it's the truth after all, why shouldn't he know it?

He was given a comfortable bed at the farm. His mother's portrait hung above it and he slept all night like a rose, horizontally; his horse slept like a block of wood, vertically, as horses do. Next morning Hopsika ate a plate of bacon and eggs and his horse ate a bag of oats. The farmer's wife brought in a scarecrow and Hopsika paid handsomely for it.

'What are you going to do with it?' she asked curiously.

'Oh,' said Hopsika, 'pay a visit to Irongrip in his fortress.'

The farmer's wife's eyes widened like saucers and she gave a screech which the cows in the byre could hear. But Hopsika doffed his hat politely, said goodbye and jumped on his horse, the portrait of his mother under one arm and the scarecrow under the other.

'Mother,' he said, 'we're going to take coffee in a stately castle. I'll be sure to behave nicely.'

And he spurred his horse in the direction of Irongrip . . .

4 Josephine

Hopsika rode away from the farm at full gallop, with the portrait under one arm and the scarecrow under the other. The path seemed even steeper than the day before, the thirteen bends even sharper, and when the fortress came in sight, high above him, its iron claws looked still more threatening.

'Oh Mother,' said the robber, 'I think perhaps you had better wait for me outside.' He hung the portrait on a tree. 'I'll be back in an hour, now.'

With the scarecrow under his arm he walked up to the wall and looked at the sharp points on the iron bars, hanging in the air above him like threatening teeth.

'Hm,' he muttered. 'Those look to me solid enough for handholds.'

He did not step right under the railings; his robber mind told him that they would clang down and he would be a prisoner.

'Off you go, scarecrow,' he murmured. 'Farewell,' and he pitched the big rag doll up at the castle wall like a fluttering bird.

The thing landed neatly on its pole and stood upright on the ground just under the wall. But almost as the scarecrow landed, like an enemy attacking with outspread arms, there was an iron squeak and the points of the railings clanged down behind the enemy and trapped him. Behind the enemy, but in front of Hopsika, who nodded appreciatively.

'Sturdy enough, indeed,' the robber repeated, 'a handy little bridge over the wall.' And like a trousered ape he clambered over the bent tops of the railings to where their hinges were made fast to the top of the wall.

'Oho!' he shouted, standing on the battlements. 'Oho, Irongrip! Here I am. Is the coffee ready?'

There was no answer and Hopsika jumped down into the stone courtyard.

'Josephine!' he cried, 'where are you? I've come to save you!'

Round and round rang the sound, and from an open door came the hollow, echoing voice: '—ave you, —ave you . . .'

Perhaps that last bit wasn't too sensible, thought the robber. Why did I do that? I've never been bothered by recklessness or bravado before. And that's the second time I've shot my mouth off.

But there was still deathly silence.

'Surely I'm not too early?' thought Hopsika. 'That would be terribly rude.'

He walked in through the open door and found himself in a long, dark stone passageway. Col*lop*, col*lop* went his boots, the stone walls magnifying the sound, and at the end of the passage were some wooden stairs. Terr*omp*, terr*omp* went Hopsika's boots on the wooden stairs, the sound echoing upwards, and he himself walking upwards, ten

steps, twenty steps, thirty, thirty-one, and then a door, standing ajar.

The robber took off his hat, knocked politely and waited for someone to call *Come in*. But no one called *Come in*. There was a shot, *clang*, and a bullet cracked the wood, close to Hopsika's hand.

'Hallo!' cried the robber. 'Have you lost your tongue?' And he flung the door wide with a crash.

There was Master Irongrip, in the middle of the room, his round belly hung with thirteen daggers and twelve pistols. Irongrip was holding the thirteenth pistol in his hand; it was still smoking.

'I said good morning!' said Hopsika with a bow. 'I must say, this——'

A second shot rang out and the bullet brushed

Hopsika's hair, because Hopsika had just dropped into a chair.

'——this is a nice place you've got here. But what *you* say sounds a little monotonous. All I can hear is *pang pang*. What does it actually mean?'

'Quite simple,' Irongrip replied grimly. 'The first *pang* means *Come in,* the second *Sit down.*' He fired a third time and the bullet whistled off in the direction of the stairs.

'That must mean *Coffee,*' said Hopsika, who was beginning to understand the pistol talk, and sure enough, a girl came in just then with a tray. The cups were tinkling and the coffee pot jiggling, the poor child's arms shook so much as she came in. Hopsika turned and looked at her.

JOSEPHINE, his robber heart told him, this must be the lovely Josephine. She had dark eyes and hair like ebony and the tatters she wore were turned to pure ermine by her figure.

Now it would have been a simple trick for Hopsika to snatch the whole tray of coffee-pot and cups and sugar and cream and fling the hot coffee with a lightning movement into Irongrip's face, sweep up Josephine and flee the fortress with her, even if a hundred men-at-arms should bar the way to him.

But Hopsika did not move a finger, because when Josephine looked at him with her great dark eyes he was paralysed by her beauty.

For just one moment.

Alas, that one moment was of fatal importance to the brave robber.

5 Lukewarm Coffee

Josephine was just stooping to put down the coffee tray when the robber was seized from behind by twenty pairs of hands. Ten men-at-arms on one side and ten on the other caught Hopsika by his arms and legs and dragged him away. They were men-at-arms in socks, otherwise Hopsika would certainly have heard them come in. What he heard now was Irongrip's grating laughter and Josephine's scream of fear as he was dragged backwards down the stairs, down still more stairs, to the deepest dungeon, into which he was flung, and clink-clank, the door was barred.

'Oh,' sighed Hopsika, 'how terribly, terribly, terribly beautiful Josephine is. Mother, if you had seen her . . .'

He climbed up to the barred window—the dungeon was not so deep, after all—and stared out. 'Ah, Mother!' he cried, 'Mother!' For he could just see her portrait which was still hanging on the tree. 'Mother, she is so sweet, as well!'

At that moment he heard a noise. The iron claws were lifted, the gates opened, hooves clattered and wheels grated on stone. A carriage came out and stopped just before the window at which Hopsika was sitting.

Irongrip stuck his ugly head out of the door. 'I'm off now,' he called to the captive robber, 'with the lovely Josephine, and I shan't be back for six months.' He grinned. 'A pity we didn't drink coffee together, but here's a cup for you.' And he threw a cup of lukewarm coffee and a biscuit through the bars. 'Just remember,' Irongrip called after it, 'this is all you're going to get to eat or drink.'

'Bah, what a mean trick,' muttered the robber. 'How cruel to kidnap that poor sweet girl!' And with tears in his eyes he stared after the departing coach.

Not till it had vanished did Hopsika pull himself together. He rubbed his clothes with his handkerchief, muttering, 'Nasty coffee, too cold and not enough sugar.' And chewing the biscuit with a grimace: 'Stale, too. Bah, what a host that Irongrip is!'

He took a look round his prison, as well as he could in the half-darkness; the stone walls were rough and damp, the ceiling low, the floor of naked rock, and there were eighteen spiders living alongside him. 'Hallo, lads,' Hopsika said to the creepy-crawlies, 'let's play a game: first out is the winner!'

He climbed up to the window again and whistled to his horse. The faithful animal was still standing under the tree by the portrait and came galloping up at once. But it had scarcely bowed its head towards the bars to look in when the iron claws fell down again with a grating screech, forming a cage all round the fortress. Now the horse was a prisoner too.

'It's a fine mechanism, though,' Hopsika had to admit. 'It works without fail. Don't be frightened, old boy,' he called to his horse, 'get hold of the scarecrow.'

For the scarecrow Hopsika had used to get in was still standing against the wall.

The faithful horse tugged the thing out of the ground with its teeth and stuck the pole through the bars. Hopsika had to undress the whole guy and pull the loose bits in one by one, and once inside, he had to put the whole thing together again. 'Well, well!' he said loudly to the scarecrow, 'well, matey, how jolly of you to look me up!' And then he shouted very loudly, in the scarecrow's voice: 'Well, what did you expect, did you think I'd leave you on your own?'

'Of course not, my dear fellow,' (in his own Hopsika-voice) 'but I'm afraid you may have to starve now with me.'

'Oh yes?' (in the scarecrow-voice) 'But what fun! We haven't done that together yet!' (loud laughter by both voices in turn).

'But look,' (Hopsika) 'seriously, my dear chap, I would have——'

Someone banged on the door. 'What does this mean?' shouted one of the men-at-arms from the passage.

'Don't disturb us!' shouted Hopsika angrily.

'What "us"?' shouted the man-at-arms. 'Surely you must be alone?'

'Ha, ha!' went Hopsika, in the scarecrow-voice, 'I'm here too, you know.'

The man-at-arms opened the hatch through which guards can look in. In the dim light of the prison he could make out the robber and beside him another figure. They bowed together; one of them rather stiffly.

'And leave us in peace now, do you hear?' said Hopsika sternly.

The guard almost fainted. He brought up his mates and let them look through the hatch one by one.

Hopsika took no notice. 'What I was going to say, my dear fellow,' he went on to his mate, 'what I was going to say was: I've discovered where Irongrip keeps his treasure hidden. It's easy to get at.'

'That's nice,' said the scarecrow, 'but it won't do you much good now. And once we've starved to death no one will know.'

'You're right about that,' Hopsika admitted. 'But after all, it wasn't all that much—a few thousand golden florins at most.'

The scarecrow shook its head, rather woodenly. 'No,' he agreed, 'scarcely worth the trouble.'

But outside the door, where the men-at-arms were listening with their ears pricked, they were dizzy with excitement. A *thousand* golden florins, they thought, and their eyes began to glitter like the gold itself. . .

6 Following the Tracks

'Hey!' cried the man-at-arms from behind the door, 'hey, where are they then, these golden florins?'

'Leave us alone!' came the angry voice of Hopsika himself. 'Please leave us to starve in peace.'

'No, no!' cried the men-at-arms, 'tell us where the treasure is and we will . . . ahum . . . we will . . .'

They stopped in confusion.

Hopsika waited.

'We'll bring you food every day.'

'Ha ha!' Hopsika the robber had to laugh at that. 'What a lot of jokers you are. Go and play cards. Good night.'

But the men-at-arms did not want to play cards, they wanted the thousand golden florins, and they began to debate whether they should let Hopsika go free if he showed them the place where the gold lay. But they didn't dare. 'We'll just cut his head off if he won't tell us,' one of them decided.

'Then he won't be able to tell us any more at all,' cried another. He was a bit brighter. But none of them was bright enough to think up a good plan.

Hopsika was. He was already working on it. He

was dressing up, while the men-at-arms were talking things over. Hopsika dressed up in the scarecrow's rags, the hat pulled down over his eyes, and the scarecrow got Hopsika's clothes, except for his boots with the silver spurs. The robber pushed those through the bars and put them in his horse's mouth. 'Hold tight, old boy, and wait for me by the gate,' he whispered.

'Hey there, you!' he shouted through the door, 'do you really want those florins badly?'

'Yes!' chorused the men-at-arms.

'Well,' said Hopsika, 'I've explained to my mate here where they are. He'll show you.'

'Good!' chorused the men-at-arms.

'But in that case you'll have to let him go,' said Hopsika. 'Then I'll go on starving here.'

'That's very nice of you,' cried the men-at arms, opening the door.

'Well, matey, all the best,' Scarecrow-Hopsika told Hopsika-Scarecrow, left leaning against the wall alone. 'Goodbye.' And with wooden steps he walked past the men-at-arms into the dim passage. 'Follow me, men,' he said in the scarecrow-voice, 'we have to go up.'

He went up the stairs with the men-at-arms behind him, sauntering along passages and through halls, past windows and arches, across the inner courtyard until he was in a low passage-way with the men-at-arms behind him.

'Here it is,' he said at last, pointing to a little room where a cupboard was standing. 'But wait a bit, let the iron claws up first, otherwise I won't be able to get out right away.' Two of the serving-men went to the gate to pull the ropes, and the others began to rummage round the cupboard.

'Wait,' said Hopsika, 'I'll get the key.' He ran out of the room, slammed the door and turned the key. Click-clack, it was locked, ha, ha!

He ran to the gate in his rags like a flapping bird. 'Quick!' he shouted to the two serving-men who had been hauling up the iron claws with the rope. 'Quick, they've already opened the cupboard. Listen to them shouting with excitement. They must have found more than a thousand in there.'

The two serving-men ran towards the room, but when they found the door locked they thought the others would not let them in to see the golden florins. There was a good deal of squabbling, and it was some time before the door was opened with the key, and the cupboard door was also forced open with swords and spears. Shelves of old helmets and rusty arrowheads and flower-pots and cobwebs and mildewed tiles and a box full of curtain rings were what they found. And one copper coin, which had rolled to the back somewhere. What a commotion they made, those men-at-arms; they turned everything upside down without finding a single golden florin. Fuming with fury they pelted down to the dungeon to cut Hopsika's head off after all, and they did it as soon as they reached him. *Crack*, it went, for Hopsika's neck was made of wood, the whole robber was made of wood with clothes on. It was not Hopsika, the only bright one realized at last.

The real Hopsika had passed through the gates long since. There he found his horse, pulled on his boots with the silver spurs, and now he was standing by the tree where the portrait of his mother hung.

'Here I am again,' he said. 'That Irongrip was a very rude fellow, you know. He gave me lukewarm coffee, and during the visit he suddenly rode off in a coach with the lovely Josephine. Can you understand people like that, Mother?'

For a moment he stared thoughtfully at the wheel-marks in the sand and a look of gloom crossed his robber's face. Then he straightened his back, cut down the portrait from the branch, put it under his arm, mounted his horse and rode down the steep path, following the tracks of the coach. At every one of the thirteen bends he sang:

'Now that I at laaast have seen
Lovely, loooovely Josephine,
To the world's end I wiiiill ride
Until I have her at myyyy side.'

He really meant it; the robber Hopsika was so terribly in love with Josephine that he could think of nothing else. Certainly not of the awful dangers into which he was now plunging with a song on his lips.

7 The Inn

The inn was made entirely of wooden planks, but all the nails were a little loose. The whole thing stood askew, like an old chest which someone has kicked in passing. Whenever the wind came whining over the plain, the inn rocked backwards, groaning on its beams, and whenever the wind turned, the whole thing tipped forwards, squeaking on its nails, as if the upstairs window wanted to look into the cellar.

'It won't fall down,' the innkeeper always assured everyone. 'What bends with the wind stands up again.' The innkeeper himself was thin and bent, and he poured the drink for his customers.

The innkeeper's wife was fat as a barrel; everything she did made her pant, and with every word she said an aitch too many. She looked after the chickens and the geese and the goats and the cats. There were twelve cats.

'Them cahats!' she panted, every time she fell over one of the twelve, and then the customers would laugh until the glasses rang. Rough folk, the customers, farmers' boys and shepherds, retired sailors and petty thieves; they drank and gambled and played cards so badly that no one ever won,

and in their rage they broke the chairs over each other's heads.

'Calm down now, lads,' the innkeeper would soothe them. 'I have to put it all together again, and that's a heap of work.'

'That Stubble!' they cried, for that was the innkeeper's name. 'Pour us another one, Stubble!' and the innkeeper poured fresh drink into the glasses so that the game could go on.

'There's Splash!' they cried to the innkeeper's wife, for that was her name. 'Going to feed the chickens, Splash?' and she said 'Yhes,' and with the tray of millet pressed to her fat tummy she pushed open the door. But she jumped in again at once, the tray of millet clattering from her hands and, panting three times as hard as before, she cried: 'A caharriage!'

That didn't often happen, a customer with enough money to arrive in a carriage. Stubble put the least broken chair ready and Splash wiped the table clean, but the customers crowded to the window to see the miracle.

It was a pitch-black carriage; a man stepped out and began to fumble with the hood as if he were going to pull out a tarpaulin. But it was not a tarpaulin, it was a set of iron bars which fitted like a cage over the whole carriage, horse and all.

'Clever,' they muttered at the window, 'that means the beast can't run away.'

They fell back as the man came towards the door. He pushed it open with a thud and thundered: 'Irongrip here! I want a full glass, a full plate and a soft bed. At once.'

Stubble came forward, bent like a reed. 'Certainly, certainly, noble sir, the best room costs ten gold——'

'Gold?' roared Irongrip. 'Ha! When I pay, I pay in steel!' He threw back his long cloak, revealing a broad belt across his stomach. In it were thirteen razor-sharp daggers. 'Steel that pricks,' he laughed menacingly, and he pushed his cloak further open to reveal a second belt with thirteen pistols in it. 'Or lead,' he added, 'lead bullets, ha ha!'

Stubble fell back, still like a reed, but quivering now. You could almost hear the quiver, it was suddenly so quiet in the inn. The rough folk looked like a flock of little lambs, face to face with a wolf. Until the silence was broken by a loud bang: Splash had fallen senseless as a sack of flour and the whole building squeaked on its nails.

'What are you waiting for?' yelled Irongrip. He now had two pistols in his hands and was shooting, *pang pang,* at a couple of glasses on the barrels, under the noses of the drinkers.

'My things!' moaned Stubble. 'Please, noble sir!' And the others pulled Splash to her feet and drove her to the kitchen to get a full dish for Irongrip, and Stubble hurried to the bedroom to make up the softest bed for Irongrip, and Irongrip himself went contentedly to the polished table to take a draught. 'They understand that language,' he muttered, grinning, 'the language of steel and lead.'

In all the hubbub no one heard the horse outside. It came click-clack along the road and on its back sat a strange being, a scarecrow, and the scarecrow wore a hat pulled down over his eyes, had a portrait under his arm, boots with silver spurs on his feet and between his lips he whistled a tune.

When he caught sight of the inn he stopped suddenly. But he was not looking at the inn; he was looking at the black carriage with the bars round it and he seemed to begin to shake a little. But only momentarily, for an instant later he jumped lithely from his horse and ran towards it.

'Psst!' called the scarecrow through the bars. 'Josephine, are you there?'

8 The Rusty Key

The window of the barred carriage was pushed down and the saddest face of the loveliest girl in the world looked out at the dark creature. 'Ooh,' she exclaimed, 'you frightened me!'

'Frightened?' he cried. 'How ridiculous! Surely you're not frightened of the robber Hopsika?'

Then she recognized his voice. 'Hopsika!' she whispered, 'what *do* you look like!'

'Yes,' said he, 'I look like something, eh? Smart suit. But I still have my boots.' He kicked up his heels one by one to show the boots with their silver spurs.

'How did you escape?' she asked. 'The dungeon was locked, wasn't it?'

'Oh yes,' said the robber, 'but Irongrip's men-at-arms thought there were two of me because I had left a scarecrow leaning against the wall outside, and I got my horse to push it in.'

'I don't understand anything,' said Josephine.

'No matter,' said Hopsika. 'I called to the men-at-arms: "My mate has come to look me up, let him out!" They did, but I had put on his clothes so they let *me* out, as the scarecrow. And that's what I still am. I've come to save you.'

'Gladly,' said Josephine. 'But how?'

'Easy,' said Hopsika. 'I'll just undo the bars.'

But the bars were not so simple to undo. They were very firmly fixed together. The robber Hopsika turned red with effort, but he could not move them an inch. 'Then I'll have to bend them apart,' he panted, 'just like a harmonica.'

But the bars were not so simple to bend apart. That cage was no harmonica and no music came out of it, although the robber Hopsika turned purple with effort.

'There's a lock on it,' said Josephine.

Hopsika looked at the lock. He stuck his little finger in the keyhole and turned, but his little finger didn't fit, neither did his index finger.

'Where is the key?' he asked.

'Irongrip has it on him,' whispered Josephine.

'Irongrip! That's true!' cried Hopsika. 'I had almost forgotten about him. Where is that unfortunate braggart?'

'Sst!' went Josephine, 'not so loud! He's there, inside the inn.'

'You should have told me at once,' said Hopsika. 'Just wait and I'll go and get the key.'

'Are you mad?' cried Josephine. 'Don't do it, Hopsika, he'll shoot you dead when he sees you.'

The robber Hopsika began to laugh heartily. 'Shoot a scarecrow dead?' he cried. 'How did you get such nonsense into your head? What good would it do him?'

Josephine stared at him, wide-eyed. The moon had risen above the roof and was shining in the great dark eyes as in two pools. It was all very beautiful and Hopsika fell silent; he even felt a little weak, like half-melted chocolate. He took the portrait, which he had set down, in his shaking hands and held it up before Josephine. 'This is my mother,' he said.

'I can't see anything,' said Josephine, for the moonlight was shining on the back of it.

'But she can see you,' said the robber. 'Isn't she beautiful, Mother?' he asked hoarsely, 'and sweet? I'm going to set her free. Now.' With the portrait under his arm he marched up to the door of the inn.

'Hopsika!' cried Josephine. It sounded like a warning. 'He'll recognize your boots!'

The robber stopped. 'She's no fool,' he thought, and with a swift movement he hung them on his horse's stirrups. 'There you are!' he waved, and now the complete scarecrow, he knocked loudly on the door, pushed it open and said: 'I say, good evening.'

It was smoky inside, and crowded, thick with the smell of frying and steamy from the drink. Glasses tinkled and deep voices droned like the hum of bees. But they all stopped at once and all eyes looked towards the door.

'Hallo, Scarecrow!' cried a deep voice, 'you've got your arms wrong. They're supposed to be stretched out!'

Hopsika put the portrait down carefully, and then, as if he were made of wood and straw, walked unsteadily with his arms outspread, towards the tables.

'Ha, ha!' laughter resounded through the inn. The rough folk thought it delightful. What a joker the fellow was! They lifted their glasses to him, the lot of them. Except for one. He did not laugh, he looked, chewing morosely, at the scarecrow and then turned his back on him.

Irongrip.

The fat man with his thirteen daggers and thirteen pistols was sitting at a separate table eating. He was eating by the plateful, brought in steaming by Splash, the innkeeper's wife, who set them, panting, before him.

''Ere you har, sir,'—fat sausages, dripping rissoles and blood-red steak—'hand pot-hatoes,' panted Splash, putting a heaped bowl of them in front of him.

Hopsika looked on with his sharp robber's eyes. 'Hey!' he cried suddenly to Stubble the innkeeper, 'that gentleman there, that gentleman is dying of thirst. He who eats much must drink much too.'

As Stubble hurried up with the bottle and Irongrip nodded approvingly, Hopsika let his gaze travel over the belts round the fat man's belly. Between the thirteen daggers in the upper belt he saw a long, rusty key.

9 A Game of Cards

Hopsika stared at the rusty key as he jogged around among the people in the inn like a scarecrow with outstretched arms. 'I've only got to snatch that thing,' he thought, 'then I can let Josephine out of the carriage-cage, and Bob's your uncle.'

He pulled his scarecrow's hat even further down over his eyes because Irongrip must not recognize him, and moved towards the table where the fat man was eating.

'Good evening,' said Hopsika with a polite bow, 'food good?'

'Clear off,' said Irongrip, waving his knife at him.

'Now, now,' said the robber, 'I'm not a leg of mutton, that's there, on your plate. You need glasses to cut with.'

Irongrip put down his knife and fork, leaned back in his chair and slowly drew one of the thirteen pistols from his lower belt.

'Aha!' cried Hopsika, 'going to do some shooting, sir. Stop your ears, lads!' The inn folk drew back, fingers in their ears, but Stubble the innkeeper came forward, moaning: 'Please, sir,' he pleaded, 'my glasses, my plates, my cups! I'll have to plaster it all again.'

'You're forgetting *me*!' cried Hopsika. 'If he shoots straight, what then? Are you going to patch me up too?'

The inn folk had taken their fingers out of their ears and they laughed uproariously.

And, of all things, Irongrip laughed too. He stuck the pistol back in his belt and laughed so loud that his fat belly shook and the thirteen daggers and thirteen pistols jingled against each other. And the rusty key jingled with them.

'How about a hand of cards?' cried Hopsika. 'Let's play forfeits.'

'And what is that?' asked the shepherd.

'Easy,' said Hopsika, 'the loser pays a forfeit; a shoe or a sock or something he has in his pocket. It's better than playing for money, because who has any money these days?'

'Yes, yes!' they cried, 'that's good! We'll do that.'

'And the gentleman can play too,' Hopsika told Irongrip. 'The gentleman has money, of course, but he can play, can't he?'

'Yes, yes!' they cried, 'that's good! We'll do that. And we'll use the pudding for forfeits.' Splash was just carrying in a floppy strawberry thing, quivering on a dish. ''Ere you h'are,' she panted. Irongrip joined in.

They all sat round a big table, their rough faces lighted by a flickering candle: the farm lad, the shepherd, the retired seafarer, the sneak-thief, the robber Hopsika and Irongrip. Stubble brought in a pack of cards and some bottles, and Splash put

the pudding in the middle of the table.

Hopsika began to shuffle the cards with his robber's fingers, and his robber's fingers arranged the aces, kings, queens and jacks exactly in accordance with his robber's plans.

'You deal,' he told the farm lad. The farm lad dealt the cards. Irongrip got nines and tens, the shepherd four aces, and Hopsika twos and threes. 'Oh,' cried the robber, 'I've lost. And the shepherd has won with four aces. Tell me what forfeit I must give.'

The old shepherd said: 'What you have in your left trouser pocket.'

'Ha, ha!' cried Hopsika, pulling a bunch of straw out of his pocket. 'Stuffing for the scarecrow.' Irongrip had to laugh and they played on. The sneak-thief shuffled, the seafarer dealt, and so it went on, all round the table.

Every time the loser had to pay a forfeit; there was a whole collection: an old hat, a bit of rope, a candle-end and a left shoe, a pipe, a tuft of sheep's wool, and then it was Hopsika's turn to shuffle again. His robber's fingers did their work and the farm lad dealt. Irongrip got twos and threes, Hopsika kings and aces.

'Well, look at me winning!' he cried in surprise, 'and who is the loser? Oh dear, Mr Irongrip, what forfeit shall I choose?'

'The pudding!' cried the people.

'Mmmm!' said Hopsika, 'that looks good,' and Irongrip looked glum, but suddenly the scarecrow seemed to take pity on him. 'Oh no,' he said, 'you eat the pudding yourself, and give me as forfeit the . . . ah, the key in your belt.'

Irongrip's hand moved to the belt round his belly, but instead of the key he grasped a dagger and rose slowly to his feet.

'No,' said Hopsika, 'I mean the *key*.'

But the inn folk grew angry. 'Cheat, cheat!' they cried. 'The gentleman can't play with us any more!'

Not play any more? That was too much for Irongrip. He sat down again, replaced the dagger, took out the key and threw it on the table. Hopsika had it for the taking, but at that very moment a violent gale blew up outside, from the east. With a ghastly screech the old inn was pushed backwards, the wooden beams, the walls and the floor heeled over, the table tipped up, with forfeits and pudding, the candle rolled spluttering right into the kitchen and deep darkness enfolded the card players, struggling, shouting and bawling on the floor.

10 Thieves in the Night

'The key,' thought Hopsika, 'the key!' But in the darkness no one could even find his own arms or legs, let alone the key. Only when Stubble the innkeeper came out of the kitchen with a new candle were they able to stand up, one after another.

'Ho,' panted Splash the innkeeper's wife, 'the mehess!'

She brought a broom and began to sweep up the splinters and the cards and the pudding and the forfeits.

'The hat's mine,' cried the farm lad. 'And that rope is mine,' said the seafarer, and everyone snatched back his property. But the key, the rusty key with which Hopsika had been going to free the lovely Josephine, did not appear among the rubbish.

'What?' fumed Irongrip, 'who has laid hands on it?'

'Perhaps hit's the cahats,' Splash suggested.

They searched the whole inn, stumbling and shouting puss, puss! But none of the twelve miaowlers had the thing. And the wind went on whining round the ramshackle building.

'Take a look here!' cried the shepherd suddenly, 'over here!' He pointed at the floor, next to the skirting. The key was stuck in the crack, but it was stuck fast, even Irongrip could not budge it.

'It squeezes hard, that wood does,' said Stubble. 'That's because of the wind; it pushes the whole thing askew and squeezes the thing together. Wait until it dies, the wind, I mean, then you can get it out with your little finger, that key there.'

There was nothing else for it, Irongrip could see. He went off to sleep in the softest bed; he did not need the key till tomorrow.

'Sleep well, sir,' said Hopsika, bowing politely.

The rest of the rough folk went out of the door, heading for home through the howling wind, and Hopsika was left alone with Stubble and Splash.

'Aren't you going home?' asked Splash.

'Ah,' said the robber, 'what would I do at home? I have no mother now.'

The innkeeper's wife laid a plump arm round Hopsika's neck. 'Ho, poor boy,' she said tenderly, 'would hyou like to sit hon my lap?'

The robber backed away politely. 'Not now,' he said, 'very kind, but there's no need.' He picked up the portrait and hung it on one of the crooked walls.

'Is that for sale?' asked Stubble.

'It is my mother,' said Hopsika, and he began to cry in chorus with the wind outside.

'Oh, poddon me,' said the innkeeper, who had received a violent shove from Splash. She stood up and pulled Stubble out to the kitchen, where the two of them began to whisper.

'Leave the stupid scarecrow in peace,' whispered Splash, 'hwhat whe whant his 'is money, 'is money!'

'He hasn't got any.'

'The rich man's, hidiot, Hirongrip's.'

'Oh, him.'

''E's not going to pay, his 'e? Then we'll 'ave to take hit. Come hon!'

And while Hopsika dozed off gradually on a chair in the taproom, the two of them crept off to the room with the softest bed where Irongrip lay snoring, and opened the door. The howling storm drowned the squeaking of the hinges, but at that very moment the clouds were torn apart and a bright stream of moonlight fell through the window onto the bed. There lay the fat man in his nightshirt, and round his nightshirt stretched the two belts. The thirteen daggers and thirteen pistols rose and fell with his breathing, glittering and gleaming in the cold light of the moon.

'Hoh,' panted Splash.

'Go carefully,' whispered Stubble.

They crept in a wide semi-circle round the bed, to the chair with the clothes on it, and began with cautious fingers to go through Irongrip's pockets.

'Ah, a gold coin!'

'Hah, two pieces hof silver.'

'Ah, a diamond!'

'Hah, a . . . pehebble!'

Splash only just stopped herself flinging the thing on the ground in a rage. That would have woken Irongrip, for it was quiet outside now. The wind had died as suddenly as it had got up. But Irongrip heard nothing.

Hopsika did. Hopsika started awake on his chair in the taproom. He had been startled by a strange sound: a shuffling, a rustling, a blowing, a—quick as a flash the robber lighted a candle and saw twelve cats leaping about on the floor as if they were fighting over something. A mouse? It clattered like iron, that was no mouse they were playing with, it was Irongrip's key. The cats had poked the key from under the skirting, where it was no longer stuck fast since the wind had died and the whole inn had straightened up.

'Puss!' went Hopsika. 'Puss, puss,' and he dived

among the fur and claws to get the key away from them.

But cats are quick and they can tease. Twelve against one they were, it was like a ball game. Twisting and turning, slithering and sliding they went across the taproom, into the passage, and then, with a harsh miaow, they shot into the room with the softest bed, where their master and mistress were busy rummaging through Irongrip's clothes.

The robber Hopsika, with one cat by the tail and one by the scruff, tripped over the threshold and fell full length on the bed, straight across Irongrip's fat belly.

One of the daggers pricked him.

11 The Iron Mouse

'Ow!' cried Hopsika. 'Do you have to do that, sir—have all those toys in bed with you?'

Irongrip woke up like a roaring lion. By the light of the moon he saw a huddle of cats on the floor, a scarecrow on his bed and the innkeeper and his wife rummaging through his clothes on the chair.

'Thieves!' he shouted, 'murderers!'

He flung Hopsika aside and drew two pistols at once in each hand.

'No, h'oh no,' panted Splash, 'don't shhoot!

Wh'e wh'ere just putting your clothes to rights. Seeing if there wh'as anything to mend or hiron, or hif there was a button missing. H'and polishing your shhoes.' She trotted out a whole litany.

'What a liar,' muttered Hopsika, crawling over the floor on hands and knees and groping among the cats under the bed.

'And you,' roared Irongrip, 'you're going to get a knife in the back!'

'Don't trouble yourself,' said Hopsika kindly, 'it's only straw, what's under my jacket. Oh, would you like to get off your bed by any chance? I can't get underneath, it dips too much in the middle.'

Irongrip turned purple in the moonlight. 'What are you doing down there?' he thundered.

'Looking,' said Hopsika. 'Ow, you beast! You scratched me.'

'What?' (Irongrip)

'These wretched cats here,' Hopsika explained. 'Their nails are much too long. Get away, you!'

'Puss, puss, puss!' called the innkeeper's wife. 'Come h'on, pussy.' She tried to slip out of the room with her puss, puss, but Irongrip pinched her fat thighs so that she fled back to the window with a yell.

'Honestly, sir,' cried Stubble, quaking, 'we didn't want your money at all. *He* was going to steal it.' He pointed his finger at the legs sticking out from under the bed.

'That's right!' Splash agreed, thinking well of Stubble's idea. 'Hand we caught 'im. Just hin time.'

'Yes!' cried Hopsika. At last he could feel the

hard, cold iron of the key among the soft fur of the cats' bodies, but just as he was going to wriggle the thing free, he was pulled from under the bed by the legs. By Irongrip. The man's hands felt like iron clamps.

'Oh, what a bore you are!' cried Hopsika. 'I shall have to begin all over again from the beginning.'

'Thief!' thundered Irongrip.

'No,' said Hopsika, 'I'm a robber. That's quite different. *They* are thieves.' He gestured towards the innkeeper and his wife. 'A pair of sneak-thieves, they are, I'm an honest robber.'

''Tisn't true!' cried the innkeeper, and: ''Tisn't true!' cried his wife.

''Tis,' said Hopsika.

''Tisn't.'

''Tis,' said Hopsika.

Irongrip's head was buzzing as if a thousand furious wasps were shut up inside it. Now he seized two daggers in each hand: 'I'll run you through, all three of you!' he shouted.

'Good idea,' said Hopsika. 'And then are you going to crawl under the bed yourself? With that fat tummy of yours? I'd really like to see that.'

Irongrip couldn't help it: he became a little bit curious. 'What's under the bed, then?' he asked.

'An iron mouse,' said Hopsika. 'The cats are playing with it.'

'You're making a fool of me!'

'Yes,' said Hopsika, 'robbers always do.'

At that moment there was a loud neighing outside. Two horses seemed to be having an argument and abusing each other roundly, trampling and scraping their hooves and scattering gravel which pattered against the window panes. Irongrip was out of bed in one leap, rushing outside in his nightshirt, a fat ghost in the pale moonlight.

What was happening was this: Hopsika's horse, which had been standing waiting obediently with Hopsika's boots on the stirrups, had moved inquisitively over to the carriage. But there it came across Irongrip's horse, and just like the first time, the two were immediately at odds. Irongrip's horse, safe under the bars of the carriage, began to kick and curse. Hopsika's horse reared and snorted back.

'Hoh, 'eavens!' cried Splash as she saw them, and she and Stubble fled to the kitchen.

Hopsika sighed with relief. 'Just let Irongrip deal with that,' he thought, and he stooped to feel among the cats under the bed. But the twelve assorted animals had rushed after Splash to the kitchen for a saucer of milk and Hopsika felt nothing.

Nothing at all? There was one thing left: the iron mouse.

'Got it,' murmured the robber.

12 Mopping Up

At last, at last, at last, Hopsika had the key in his hand! Josephine could be released from the barred carriage. But when he ran into the taproom to get outside, Irongrip came menacingly to meet him in the doorway. In his hand he held Hopsika's boots, the silver spurs glittering in the light of the rising sun.

'Now I know who you are, Scarecrow,' hissed Irongrip. 'I know these boots.'

'It's high time,' said Hopsika, smiling. 'Good morning, Mr Irongrip,' and he politely removed his scarecrow's hat.

'Blackguard!' roared Irongrip. 'How did you escape from my prison?'

'Oh,' said Hopsika, 'that's one of the robber's trade secrets. Let me pass and I'll just get Josephine out of the carriage. The poor child must be hungry . . .'

Irongrip drew two pistols.

'. . . and have slept badly,' Hopsika went on. 'A good breakfast will do her good.'

Irongrip pointed the pistols at Hopsika's heart.

'How clever,' mocked the robber, 'at such close range. I know something better.' He placed the key on his head and held it upright by the ring. 'Try to shoot through that,' he said. 'That would be much nicer.'

Irongrip took another step forward, hissing.

'*Still* closer?' cried Hopsika. 'Is your shooting that bad?'

'Give that key here,' roared Irongrip.

'Here you are,' said Hopsika and, stretching out his arm he handed over the key, but just as Irongrip was about to snatch it, Hopsika threw it high in the air and caught it with his other hand. At the same time he ducked his head between Irongrip's legs and jerked upright, so that the fat-belly flew through the room in an arc and landed on the bar counter like a sack of garbage. Eleven glasses and two bottles fell in tinkling fragments, and a beer cask rolled over so that the brown liquid surged foaming across the floor.

'My property, my property!' moaned Stubble, coming out of the kitchen with Splash behind him.

'A mhop!' she panted. 'A buhucket and a mhop. The place his flooded.'

But the robber Hopsika walked out, whistling. He had scooped up his boots with the silver spurs, which had also flown across the taproom. He put them on and went up to the carriage.

'Josephine,' he cried brightly, 'I have the key here, I've come to let you out.'

'Ooh,' came faintly from behind the windows.

With quivering fingers Hopsika put the rusty key in the rusty lock of the fence of bars. It sprang open with a groan and——

'Mother!' cried Hopsika. 'Oh dear, oh dear, Josephine. Wait a minute, I was just about to forget my mother! I was just going to leave her in suspense. How awful, how awful!' With tear-filled eyes he rushed back into the inn to fetch the portrait which he had hung on the crooked wall.'

'Mother,' he cried, sobbing, as he pushed the door open, 'Mother, don't be cross with me, I——'

But the painting was not there. Not on the crooked wall; only the empty nail was there. 'How, where——' cried the robber, and turned about, his face pale as death.

Stubble, behind the counter, peered at him with half-closed eyes. Splash, beside him, was holding the portrait in her fat arms and smiling slyly. 'Pick up the bhroom,' she panted roughly, 'hand swheep hup the mess.' Hopsika walked slowly up to her.

'Stay where you are,' she cried, 'hor hI'll scratch!'

Her long nails moved threateningly right in front of the beautifully painted face in the portrait. Hopsika froze. 'If you do *that* . . .'

'Swheep,' she ordered. 'Hall the pieces. And mhop. Hall the beer. Nice and neatly now.'

The robber Hopsika picked up the broom and began to sweep the splinters of the eleven broken glasses, rinkle-tinkle together, sloshing about in the spilt beer. Stubble and Splash watched. 'Here's another bit, there's another bit,' they pointed out from time to time.

'Oh Mother,' sighed Hopsika, 'I'm doing it for you.'

Then he took the mop and, bending down, began to mop up the beer from the wooden floor. So much had been spilt that it rippled. Mopping as he went past Stubble's feet, past Splash's feet, he reached the door, and there, wide apart, stood the feet of Irongrip. The fat man's thunderous laugh made Hopsika's heart shrink.

'Goodbye,' cried Irongrip, 'thanks for the forfeit, otherwise the iron mouse, in short, the key.' He stumped away with heavy tread, and a moment later came the rattle of carriage wheels dying slowly away in the distance.

'Josephine,' went Hopsika. 'Oh Mother, she is so beautiful . . .' and he wrung the mop out in the bucket.

Hopsika mopped up twelve bucketfuls of beer and only then did he get the portrait back. Whistling glumly, he mounted his horse to follow in the tracks of the carriage once again. Behind him a puff of wind sent the inn sagging to the left with the piteous screech of a thousand nails, as if the building were staring sympathetically after him. Then the robber suddenly had to laugh and his whistle became merry.

'I *will* get her,' he murmured.

13 Atsabootsa

Atsabootsa was a place of pleasure. There were twelve fairs and five circuses there, eighty hot-dog stalls, seventy-seven rifle ranges and in the middle of the big square, a Try-your-Strength machine with a forty-nine-pound hammer. Anyone who scored a triple-ringer with it could eat and drink for nothing all evening, and sleep in a soft feather bed.

In Atsabootsa there were seven hundred ale-houses, six hundred wine bars, five hundred lemonade tents, sixty gaming tents where you could bet and play cards and solve puzzles, fifty merry-go-rounds and one graveyard. For even in Atsabootsa people died—in spite of all the fun.

That churchyard was a dark place and the gallows stood beside it, but otherwise there was always light everywhere in the city of Atsabootsa. From the sun by day, from the ninety thousand multi-coloured oil lamps by night, lit by the inhabitants themselves: two lamps each, or sometimes three, if there were many sick.

The city of Atsabootsa lay over the mountains, beside a dark blue lake filled by the great river which came thundering and foaming down the final slope. And one day the robber Hopsika came clattering down at least as fast, galloping on his horse, on the tracks of the carriage. The robber reined in his horse at the gates of Atsabootsa, to let it steam off and to collect his own thoughts.

'Mother,' he said, unhooking the portrait of the dear old lady from his saddle, 'Mother, they have entered the city. That windbag Irongrip has dragged my lovely Josephine off to the city of fun. Now she will have to gamble and play cards and drink along with that blustering Irongrip. I have to save her, more than ever now.'

He was about to hang the portrait on his horse again, but the eyes seemed to be saying something. 'No, Mother,' cried Hopsika, 'honestly, I promise not to join in their wickedness. I shan't gamble or play cards or even drink—well, perhaps just a little lemonade, not even fizzy—I'll simply look around until I find the rogue and the darling.'

When Hopsika rode through the gates of Atsabootsa the fun was in full swing. He had scarcely taken the second street on the right when he landed in the midst of a group of jigging people, who were singing loudly:

'In Atsabootsa, bright and glad,
All the bars are full, my lad
Full of wine and full of beer,
And you, my lad, are full of cheer.'

'Hey, Scarecrow!' they called to Hopsika, 'how sour you look. Get down off that nag and dance with us.'

Scarecrow, thought Hopsika. I haven't even changed yet. He jumped off his horse, tied it up on the grass, dived into a secondhand clothes shop and reappeared as a robber.

'That's better!' cried the fun-people. 'Now we'll teach you to dance.'

'Not a bit of it,' said Hopsika. 'I'm looking for a carriage with a fat man in it and a beautiful girl.'

'Ha, ha!' they cried, 'you'll find those everywhere here, come along.'

Hopsika waved to his horse and followed the dancing people. One-two-three, one-two-three and a hop they danced, and the robber's long legs could not keep walking demurely along. In no time they had joined in with a one-two-three hop and at the next turning Hopsika's whole body was joining in, bowing and twisting, turning and swaying.

'That's right!' cried the Atsabootsers. 'Hup-two-three, hup-two-three!' And the robber Hopsika danced through the streets with the portrait of his mother in his arms, as if she were still a living woman. Round they went, round and round, and then inside somewhere where everything went on turning in front of his eyes, people and tables and chairs and glasses, and glasses were pressed into his hands, two at once, and dancing, he drank them down.

'Lovely fizzy lemonade!' cried Hopsika.

'Ha, ha!' they laughed, 'joker!' For it was beer.

'What about the carriage?' cried Hopsika. 'Where is the carriage now, with the fatso in it?'

'Ha, ha,' they cried, 'here, right under your nose!' And they pointed to the bar counter, with the barrel of an innkeeper behind it.

But Hopsika was not looking. When the spinning in front of his eyes stopped his glance fell on a big round table in the middle of the ale house. A gambling table.

There were six people sitting round it, staring with red, excited faces at the little ball rolling to and fro, and in the middle stood the pot—a pot full of clinking silver coins.

Hopsika's eyes began to shine.

'One moment, Mother,' whispered the robber and he set the portrait down carefully, facing the wall, so that she could not see what he was doing.

14 The Gaming Table

The six men who were gambling had each drawn a circle in chalk on the table and written some figures it it. The ball rolled about until it stopped in one of the circles.

'What a childish game,' Hopsika began as he made his way towards it. 'Is ten the highest?'

The men looked up. 'Like a hundred, would you?' asked one.

Hopsika began to laugh. 'Nothing less than a thousand,' he said.

'Braggart,' cried another. 'If you lose you have to put a thousand in the pot.'

'Is that all?' asked Hopsika. 'I'll join in then.'

Now it was the eyes of the six which began to shine. 'Great!' they cried as Hopsika sat down beside them. 'The seventh player is always lucky,' he said, 'tra la la!' and he drew a big chalk circle on the table, with the figure 1000 inside it. 'Get going with that ball!' It rolled and rolled to and fro across the table, over the 10 circle and 50 circle and back past the 30 circle and then Hopsika gave the table a sly nudge with his knee so that the ball rolled towards the 1000 circle. Hopsika had drawn the last nought very thick, it was an absolute bank of chalk and the ball stuck neatly in it.

'Lucky dog!' cried the men, their eyes popping out.

'Oh, that's only the beginning,' said the robber, emptying the pot of silver tinkle-tinkle into his pockets. 'Next round!'

The six players sat there with their mouths open.

'Haven't you got any more money?' asked Hopsika in surprise. 'What a shabby sort of place this is.'

'*We* have, *we* have!' cried the others in the ale house. They crowded round the table, gamblers with glittering eyes, the pot was filled with more silver, fresh rings were drawn, with 100 and 500 inside them, and Hopsika made a fresh ring too, with 10,000 in it and a still thicker band of chalk. The little ball rolled, Hopsika nudged, slyly, slyly, with his knee and whoops! it stuck on the 10,000.

'Lucky dirty dog!' shouted the players.

'Oh,' said Hopsika, 'a million would be nice, of course, but I'm sure you haven't got that?'

No, they hadn't got that. The gambling tent almost burst apart with the fury of all the people who had lost their gambling money.

'Well,' said Hopsika, 'I'll go and look for it somewhere else. Good evening, everyone.' He picked up the portrait and walked out, tinkling as if he himself were the pot of silver.

A dark figure stole out of the ale house behind him.

'Oh Mother, Mother,' sighed the robber, 'what have I done? I daren't face you. But I'll make it up to them, at once, I'll spend it all again.'

He ran to a roundabout, paid double and whirled round with the portrait in his arms. 'Don't get sick now, Mother.'

From the helter-skelter to the slippery pole, from the slippery pole to the roller-coaster, and everywhere he paid twice. And everywhere the dark figure followed him.

From the roller-coaster to the haunted house, with windows glowing green, where cobwebs stroked your face and screams came from all sides. 'Don't be frightened, Mother, it's not real.'

He went right through the fairground with the portrait and the dark figure from the ale house stole after him, but at the last roundabout the dark figure laid a hand on Hopsika's shoulder.

'Cheat,' he lisped, 'I thaw you. Nudging it with your kneeth.'

Hopsika turned round.

'You mutht hand over half your money,' lisped the man, 'or I'll go to the polithe.'

'Good idea!' cried Hopsika. 'Go at once!' He grasped the lisper by the scruff, whirled him round his head at the speed of a merry-go-round and then let go. 'My compliments to the polithe!' cried the robber.

Like a cannon ball the dark figure flew through the air, landed on one of the circus tents, tore a hole in it and fell into the sawdust of the ring among the clowns. The public bellowed, but Hopsika did not. He walked dizzily on through the fun-city of Atsabootsa—what was it he was looking for?—and at last he came to the great central square where the Try-your-Strength machine stood. The enormous forty-nine-pound hammer lay beside it and the Try-your-Strength man stood by, shouting.

'Who'll have a go?' he shouted in his fairground voice. 'Who's going to give it a bang?' He pointed to a wooden head, flattened by the hammer blows. When you hit it a lead weight slid up a pole. Halfway up it rang a bell, still higher a second bell and, at the top, the winning third bell. 'No one can strike a three-ringer!' the man shouted. 'No one has ever won free drinks and the soft feather bed. Ha, ha, most people can't even pick up the hammer!'

Hopsika stopped. A whole circle of people had stopped. Then came a voice, a deep voice: 'Here!' rumbled the voice. 'Hand over the hammer. A soft feather bed, that's for me.' A big, fat, heavy man pushed his way forward.

Irongrip. . . .

15 Try-Your-Strength

The crowd standing round the Try-your-Strength machine gazed awe-struck at the burly man who stepped forward.

'Just you hand over that toy hammer, little fellow,' the fat man thundered to the owner of the machine.

The crowd backed respectfully, except for Hopsika, who had just caught sight of the lovely Josephine. She was standing with her beautiful eyes cast down, just behind Irongrip, like a captive rabbit which does not dare to run away when it is set free.

Irongrip swung the forty-nine-pound hammer through the air like a feather, and then, arm muscles bulging, he brought the thing down on the wooden head. The crash was deafening, the lead weight shot right up the pole, two bells rang out over the square, followed a second later by the third bell, the top one. The highest point had been reached, a rare occasion.

'Hurrah!' cried the crowd (except for Hopsika) and 'Free drinks!' cried the owner, 'and the soft feather bed for the gentleman!'

'Ha,' sneered Irongrip, 'a mere trifle for my strength. Here!' he tensed his arm muscles into thick steel cords and displayed them to the crowd. 'Who's going to match me now, eh? Bunch of weaklings!'

The crowd backed further.

Hopsika stayed where he was.

'Dear me,' said the robber, shaking his head. 'I can do a bit better than that.'

Irongrip did not seem to have noticed him until then.

'Better?' he thundered, turning red, 'you skinny weed, would you—hey young shaver, I know you!

Aren't you the floor-sweeper from the ale house who——'

'Yes,' said Hopsika, 'that's right. What a memory, what a memory! I would never have thought it with all those muscles. Generally a head like yours is full of sawdust.'

A suppressed snigger from the crowd, who had shuffled forward again, sent the angry purple into the bruiser's cheeks.

'Sprat!' he cursed. 'Braggart! I'll fill your head full of lead.' He drew two pistols at once and the crowd pressed back, screaming. Except for Hopsika. He stayed where he was.

'Easy,' said the robber calmly. 'Everyone's going to admire you for your nifty pistol work: two at once, at a range of one metre. Dear me!'

Josephine, who had now recognized Hopsika as well, had turned deathly pale. From behind Irongrip's broad back she looked at him, shaking her dead desperately.

But Hopsika nodded back with a smile, so that Irongrip dropped his pistols helplessly.

'That's good,' said Hopsika. 'Now just you give me that hammer and we'll see what we shall see.'

The robber stooped and put the portrait of his mother against a post so that she could see what he was doing. The crowd shuffled forward again and the owner of the Try-your-Strength, still trembling with fright, handed Hopsika the hammer. Forty-nine pounds is quite a lot, and the robber staggered under its weight. Irongrip, looking on, legs set wide, began to roar scornfully.

'Ha, ha, what a weakling!' Suddenly Irongrip

was having fun, he regarded the stagger as weakness, but Hopsika was aiming carefully, very carefully. Not much strength was needed, that hammer simply had to fall, not on the wooden head, no, in another place. And so it did: forty-nine pounds of iron landed straight on the toes of the unsuspecting Irongrip.

There was no bell, let alone three of them; there was a dull thud, followed by a roar something like an 'ouch!' Irongrip danced round on one leg like an inflated stork, clutching his injured foot in both hands.

This time the crowd, instead of backing, burst into peals of laughter. Except for Hopsika. The robber was not laughing. He dropped the hammer, shot forward, caught Josephine by the arm and drew her away.

'Soak it in ice-cold water!' he called back to Irongrip. 'Put that foot in a bucket of ice-cold water, it will reduce the swelling.'

But scarcely had Hopsika taken a few steps with the lovely Josephine on his arm when his other arm was gripped, as if in a vice.

'I arrest you in the name of the law of Atsabootsa,' came a harsh voice in his ear. One policeman, two, three policemen, with tall helmets on their heads, formed a ring about him.

'Yeth!' lisped a voice. 'That'th him, the rathcal who cheated. He won himthelf millionth of thilver pietheth with hith nudging. I thaw him mythelf!'

The dark lisper from the ale house stood there, the false betrayer, who had brought in the police in order to revenge himself on Hopsika.

'This is a nice thing,' muttered the robber, forced to let Josephine go again. 'Don't lose heart, dearest,' he whispered to her, and looking round he cast a glance at the portrait.

'Mother, I have to leave you behind now too,' he cried, but the portrait seemed to be giving him a mischievous wink.

16 Hunted Through the Town

The policeman's hands were clamped on Hopsika's arm, but when he saw the portrait's naughty wink the robber suddenly came to life. Like lightning he raised his left boot and dug the policeman in the side with the silver spurs.

'Ooh, that tickles!' the man cried, wriggling, and his grip on Hopsika's arm slackened. The robber wrenched himself free, ducked between the other policemen, snatched his mother's portrait, blew a kiss to Josephine and disappeared like an eel in the crowd.

'Catch him!' yelped Irongrip who was still hobbling round on one leg.

'Thtop thief!' cried the lisper: and, 'Stop or I'll shoot!' ordered the policeman.

Hopsika had to laugh as he ran. The pursuit began.

'Let's see what they can do,' thought the robber,

jumping into a fairground car. All the policemen jumped after him into other fairground cars.

'Pay up!' cried the owner, 'pay up, the lot of you!' But Hopsika nipped out and whipped into the ghost house, and all the policemen nipped and whipped after him, except for one, who found ghosts too spooky.

'Booh!' yelled Hopsika in the pitch darkness, and he hid behind the green window until they had all passed. Then he went out again through the entrance, but there stood the one scared policeman, who shouted: 'Catch him, here he is!'

The hunt went on.

Hopsika ran into the waffle tent and overturned the oil pan so that all the policemen skidded and fell on their noses. After that he flew like a whirlwind straight through one of the gaming tents, snatching up some silver as he went, and ran up the street.

'Catch him! Catch the thief!'

The streets of the fun-town of Atsabootsa were like a maze. My horse, thought Hopsika, I must find my horse, somewhere near the gate—but all the streets ran in different directions, which Hopsika did not know, and the policemen did. They took shorter routes and gained on him steadily, more and more, and in a little square where a big wheel stood they almost got him. Hopsika took a tremendous leap into the air and grabbed one of the gondolas of the Big Wheel so that he was carried upwards with it. Up he rose, his long booted legs dangling, higher and higher.

'Aha!' cried the police, 'don't worry, men, he'll

be coming down by himself on the other side.' They got ready, but Hopsika did not come down. He had climbed into the gondola and was jumping from one to the next like a lithe cat, high above the ground.

'Lovely view up here!' he shouted down to the policemen. And he could easily see now where the gate lay and where his horse was standing. 'Hang on, Mother. Don't get dizzy now.'

But then two of the policemen jumped into the gondola: we'll get at the rascal that way, they thought cunningly, and they were right. Hopsika saw them sitting there with fierce expressions, on the swaying seat.

'Hey, there!' he called down to the owner of the Big Wheel, 'there's another two who haven't paid! They haven't got tickets!'

'What?' called the owner, and he made the wheel turn back so that he could catch the defaulters.

A row started up below and Hopsika allowed himself to slide cautiously along the spokes of the wheel to the ground and fled.

'Catch him!'

The chase began anew, but now Hopsika knew the way and soon got rid of them in the twisting streets, until at last the robber was safely back with his horse.

'Hey, hey, Mother,' he sighed, 'here we are again.' He hung the portrait on the saddle, jumped onto the horse and galloped to the gates. But they were shut. Shut tight. With an oak door and iron bars.

'How tiresome they are in Atsabootsa,' sighed

the robber. 'Now I shall have to spend all night in the place, with all that fairground noise. Bah!' He tied his horse up again and went in search of a quiet bed. He found one after a time, simply by climbing through a window, wriggling his long body like a worm. He found himself in a pleasant passage, in a still pleasanter room, and there was a splendid bed, covered with soft pillows.

Hopsika pulled off his boots, rubbed the silver spurs till they shone, put them down and stretched out. 'Oh, how nice,' murmured the robber, and he yawned and fell into a deep sleep.

17 Pillow Fight

Hopsika's sleep was not only deep; it was also full of dreams. The Try-your-Strength had Irongrip's head in it and he was bashing it with the forty-nine-pound hammer, scoring a three-ringer, but Irongrip laughed thunderously and Josephine gave a shrill scream. Hopsika was woken by the scream, the Try-your-Strength machine was right on top of him, but it was Irongrip, fat and heavy and real. 'Now I've got you, little man, you won't escape me again,' thundered Irongrip, and he drew two flashing daggers from his belt.

Hopsika yawned loudly. 'Hey,' he said, 'I was just having such a beautiful dream.'

'In *my* bed!' hissed Irongrip. He raised the daggers high, their points aimed at the robber.

It was no dream now, Hopsika could see that clearly, and the bed he was lying on (he could see that now too) was that very bed of soft feathers meant for the winner of the three-ringer blow: Irongrip.

'Don't be cross with me,' said the robber. 'I thought I ought to warm it up for you.'

'Skunk!' cried Irongrip, quivering with fury.

'Certainly not,' said Hopsika, 'I'm a nice hot water bottle. You mustn't prick it with those knives, it would leak and your whole bed would get wet.'

Josephine stood, pale as death, by the door—pale and yet beautiful.

'*Arggh!*' roared Irongrip. 'Then I'll have to stab you beside the bed.'

'That would be best,' Hopsika agreed. 'Get off me, then. You're squashing me so tight I can't move.'

Irongrip had to get up. With the daggers held threateningly he stood upright and remained beside the bed.

'Ooh,' sighed Hopsika, 'that's a relief!' He yawned loudly once again and rubbed his eyes. 'I'm not fully awake yet,' he said. 'It's so early, you see.' He moved as if to turn over, but suddenly he shot up, draped in sheets and blankets like a ghost, and screamed: '*Brooah!*'

'*Arggh!*' thundered Irongrip, stabbing with two daggers at once, but he stabbed the pillow which Hopsika was holding in front of him so that the white down flew into the air, and Hopsika said 'Peep-bo!'

It was a crazy fight, with bedclothes flapping across the room, sometimes with Hopsika inside them, sometimes without. 'Peep-bo!' cried the robber, 'peep-bo' here, 'peep-bo' there, and fat Irongrip staggered around on his fat legs, stabbing

sheets and blankets till they lay in ribbons on the floor. And at each stab Hopsika cried 'Coo-ee, that wasn't me!'

Irongrip wore himself out. His head looked like a red cabbage, for he had eaten a lot and drunk a lot, and his foot still hurt where Hopsika had hit it with the hammer.

'Josephine!' cried Hopsika, leaping to and fro, 'quick, run to the town gates and wait for me by my horse. I'm just coming.'

She understood him and vanished through the door like a shadow. Irongrip gave a roar of rage which startled half the fun-city of Atsabootsa.

And that was a pity, because when Hopsika finally threw the feather mattress over Irongrip and slipped backwards out of the door, he was grabbed there by seven policemen at once. One caught him by his hair, one by his throat, two by his arms, two by his legs and the last by his trouser belt.

'March!' he heard.

The robber had no defence. He let himself be dragged away like a limp dishcloth, down the passage, out of the house, along the winding street, straight to the prison of Atsabootsa with its thick, thick bars.

'Tomorrow you'll be dangling from the gallows!' cried the seven policemen, barring the doors *crick-crack* behind him, and their echoing laughter died away down the corridor.

'Dear me,' muttered the robber, 'and all this time that poor girl is waiting for nothing.'

He took a look out, but all he could see were the feet of the passers-by.

'Mother,' he thought, 'it's lucky I left you hanging from the saddle. Josephine can look after you.'

His eyes began to swim with tears a little at the thought, and mistily he saw a pair of little feet stop by the barred window.

'Hey, there!' cried Hopsika hoarsely, 'listen a moment!'

Knees appeared and then a head: a little lad.

'Here,' said Hopsika, 'here's a silver piece for you. Go to the gate and you'll find a pretty girl and a horse. Tell her not to wait any longer. Tell her to escape on my horse.' The urchin nodded, took the silver piece and vanished.

'And look after the portrait!' the robber called after him.

The footsteps began to run and died away.

Hopsika sat down on the straw and began to sing softly and rather sadly to himself:

'My lovely Josephine, adieu,
while here I die of sorrow;
yearning for one more glimpse of you
before I hang tomorrow.'

18 The Last Wish

Hopsika was singing a sad song in the straw of his cell, but in Atsabootsa, the fun-town, they made even the hanging of a robber into a party. A huge procession, with drums and trumpets and flags and banners and people in costume and skipping children, moved through the streets on the way to the gallows beside the churchyard.

Hopsika was taken from the prison and had to walk in the procession wearing the rope round his neck like a dog on a lead, with the people of Atsabootsa shouting: 'Nasty robber!' after him, and 'Cheat!' and 'Lazy layabout!'

Hopsika laughed back cheerfully. 'Pooh!' he cried, 'is that all? I've done far worse things than that!' and he blew the girls of Atsabootsa kisses which made them blush, whether they would or no, for the robber had such a mischievous freckled face, and they thought him much nicer than the dull fellows with whom they went eating waffles every evening.

The gallows stood on a mound; Hopsika had to climb up it and all the people stood round it.

'Just like a play!' cried Hopsika. 'Ladies and gentlemen, pay attention!' He began to do crazy dance steps and pull faces with his freckled face. 'When I dieee . . . !' he sang, but the hangman tugged at the rope round his neck and said he must keep quiet.

'Oh, beg pardon,' cried Hopsika. 'Ladies and gentlemen, I started too soon.'

The people had to laugh, and the judge shouted for silence because he was going to read out the verdict.

'The robber Hopsika,' he began, 'has been found guilty of cheating, riding in fairground cars for nothing, hitting someone on the toes with a hammer . . .' Hopsika was not listening; the whole story of his misdeeds was read out like a dreary history lesson, and he knew it already. His eyes wandered over the crowd, he saw the dark lisper who had betrayed him, grinning in the front row, and the owner of the Try-your-Strength and then, suddenly, a shock went through Hopsika. There stood Josephine, beautiful Josephine, and beside her his horse, with the portrait of his mother on the saddle. Had she not escaped? Had she been unable to leave him in the lurch? He saw her waving and he waved back, and his robber's heart began to beat like a madman's. Just wait, he thought.

'. . . condemned to be hanged,' the judge ended his dreary recital.

The hangman threw the rope over the gallows and was about to pull, but Hopsika said: 'Whoa, wait a minute, that won't do.'

'What's 'at?' asked the hangman.

'My last wish,' said Hopsika. 'I'm allowed to make a last wish, that's part of an execution.'

'Hmm,' said the judge. 'That's true, hangman, one moment please. What's it to be, Robber?'

'My boots,' said Hopsika. 'I should very much like to be hanged with my boots on. They're still under the feather bed.'

The hangman had to go and fetch them and, meanwhile, Hopsika pulled such funny faces for the public that everyone, even Josephine, had to burst out laughing. All except the ferret-faced lisper.

'Here you are!' The hangman, panting from his run, flung the boots down in front of Hopsika. The robber pulled them on and the silver spurs flashed in the sunlight, razor-sharp.

'Ready!' called Hopsika. 'Pull away!'

A sigh ran through the crowd, for it really was a shame about this nice fellow with the freckles, and Josephine began to sob. Only the portrait of Hopsika's mother smiled and winked, but no one saw it, because everyone was looking at the dangling robber.

Dangling?

Well, no—Hopsika's feet had not left the ground before he swung them up—*hoopla,* performed a neat flip on the rope as if he were at a gym display, and cut right through it with his razor-sharp silver spurs. He landed on hands and feet, sprang up, gave the hangman a shove, leaped from the platform, slid like a cat between the people to the place where Josephine stood, seized her under the arms and leaped with her into the saddle—no, the leap was not completed, because she was heavy and fat and . . . it *wasn't* Josephine—it was Irongrip.

Ugly, loathsome, fat, ungainly, cursed Irongrip, who had come stumbling up, limping on his painful toes, just as Hopsika performed his beautiful flip, and had moved into Josephine's place.

With a cry of disgust Hopsika let the fat muscle-man go, jumped into the saddle alone and raced, hell for leather, through the streets and out of the gate, away from Atsabootsa, the city of pleasure. Away from Josephine, who was in Irongrip's power again . . . .

And, as he fished the bullets which Irongrip had fired after him out of his hat, Hopsika told the portrait aloud:

'Mother, Mother, I really shall get her one day!'

19 The Black Ghost

High in the mountains lay the ruins of an old castle. The windows looked like gaping holes in a skull, where the wind moaned through, but one tower was still standing, waggling in the wind like a wounded finger which seemed to beckon.

But no shepherd dared to go anywhere near the ruin. Old Farandol, great-grandson of the French major who had been hidden in the hay-stack at Lammers for three years, said the ruins were haunted.

'Smoke comes out of them,' he used to say scratchily. 'And a reddish glow. I saw it again last night.'

'Oh yes?' said Berto and Berti, who did not really believe him—they were still too young.

But their elder sister Berta, who spent her whole life stringing beans, said that two whippersnappers like them must shut their ears to ghost stories.

'I keep my sheep away from there too,' said Farandol. 'The white williewaws lie in wait for them. I've already lost two beasts.'

'Nonsense,' said Berta. 'What could ghosts do with sheep?'

'Eat them,' suggested Berto.

'Suck their blood,' mused Berti.

'Bed,' said Berta. She tipped the beans into a saucepan full of water.

The boys went to their room and straight out again through the window, to climb the hill in the twilight. 'There's no harm in looking,' they said, but above them the wind howled through the empty windows and they stopped among the bushes at a distance.

Nothing happened; even the wind died down, whispering through the leaves, and the crickets chirped so merrily that Berto and Berti fell asleep.

Watch out! In the pitch darkness they were startled awake by a nervous bleating. The grey form of a sheep came tripping past the bushes and a light shone from the ruins. A red glow, full of twisting smoke, and in the glow they saw two ghostly figures roughly pulling the sheep inside.

Their eyes popping out with terror, Berto and Berti ran back to the hut and jumped back through the windows into bed, right under the blankets.

'Of course,' said Berta next morning, 'of course you dreamed about ghost stories. You ought to have shut your ears.'

But Farandol came in, counting on his fingers: 'thirty-eight, thirty-nine, forty – wrong,' he said. 'Little Mary has gone.'

Berta snapped a bean in two. '*That* sheep?' she said. 'Oh well, it only had a moth-eaten coat.'

'We saw it, we saw it!' cried Berto and Berti. 'That was Little Mary. She was baaing.'

The boys told their story again and Farandol decided to keep watch.

But nothing happened the next night, nor the

night after that.

'You see?' said Berta.

But Little Mary did not come back and on the third night Berto was woken by Berti clicking his fingers. 'Listen!'

Baaing, bleating and trampling.

The boys flew outside and up the stony path to the meadow where old Farandol was sitting by the watch-fire.

'Trouble,' hissed the shepherd. 'The flock can smell it—stay *here* Cornelia—the wool is curling on their backs for fear. Listen!'

But the ruin loomed black against the twinkling starry sky and the tower finger did not move. No glow to be seen, no smoke, and the plaintive moaning was only the wind in the empty windows.

Or was it?

Was that a black figure, appearing up there? A ghost in night-attire, softer and stealthier than smoke?

'Who's there?' Farandol cried, hoarsely but bravely.

Footsteps. Not the trample of sheep or bleating, but slowly approaching footsteps, an iron sound as of an iron-shod knight kicking against stones in the grass.

Farandol backed. Berto and Berti backed still further. In the flickering light of the watch-fire a great head reared up, with pointed ears, a long hairy neck, a back, and on its back a black ghost, wearing a hat.

'*Whoops!*' they heard.

The ghost floated to the ground, with an

ordinary jump, and stepped into the ring of light.

'Can I have a warm-up?' he asked. 'And my horse? We're both cold. Oh, and Mother too.' He unhooked a large portrait from the saddle and thoughtfully held it close to the fire.

Ghost?

It was only the robber Hopsika.

20 A Dismal Story

It was some time before the shepherd family recovered from their fright, but then old Farandol pounced.

'I know you!' he cried. 'I know you from the crooked inn. You cheated at cards there.'

'That's right,' said Hopsika. 'Shall we play another hand?'

'Grab him, boys!' cried Farandol. 'He's still got a tuft of wool of mine as a forfeit.'

Berto and Berti jumped up nervously, still trembling from their ghost fright, and grasped Hopsika by the shoulders.

The robber stayed calmly where he was. 'Give a thought to my mother,' he said. 'See she doesn't fall in the flames.'

'Hand over the tuft,' said old Farandol, flourishing his shepherd's crook.

'I'll give you a couple of gold pieces,' said

Hopsika amiably. 'Let me go now, boys.'

'Don't do it! He's dangerous. Where do you come from, miserable sheep thief?'

Hopsika looked at the old man with tired eyes. 'How unkind,' he said. 'I steal gold and silver, but not dear little sheep. Never.'

'Ha,' said Farandol, clearing his throat. 'You came from the ruins and you stole Little Mary. And Corrie and Bella.'

'But my dear sheep-man,' cried Hopsika, 'I have come from the fairground, from the roundabouts of Atsabootsa. Little Mary and Corrie and What's-her-name are nothing to do with me. Only Josephine, my lovely, sweet——' He began to sob quietly.

Berto and Berti felt the robber's shoulders shaking, and the portrait almost fell into the flames.

Now Farandol had a good heart, and a good heart feels for the pangs of love. Robber or no robber, Hopsika must come to the hut with them and have some hot soup.

They sat round the table, the old shepherd, Berto, Berti and even Berta, who left her green beans alone while Hopsika told his story.

'I am an honest robber,' he began. 'Aren't I, Mother?' (The portrait of the old lady was hanging behind his chair.) 'Everything I steal I give honestly back again, or to the poor, but now I have to steal back the lovely Josephine. She was imprisoned in Irongrip's fort, and he is a bad knight with an ugly pot-belly; he took her away in a carriage with bars, but I escaped from the fortress as a scarecrow and caught up with them at the crooked inn. There I almost had Josephine in my arms—oh, she is so sweet and lovely—but Irongrip rode away with her under my very nose, to the fun-town of Atsabootsa, and there I struck the evil pot-belly on the toes with the Try-your-Strength hammer, but then I had to go to the gallows, while Josephine——'

'That's enough,' said Berta. She did not like love stories. She went back to her beans, *snap snap*, as if she were breaking hearts.

'Did they string you up?' asked Berto.

'On a real hangman's rope?' asked Berti.

'Indeed they did, boys,' said Hopsika. 'For a moment. Then I did a flip and cut through the rope, *whoops* with my silver spurs, but Josephine, oh . . . Josephine.'

Snap snap went Berta's beans, and suddenly Hopsika straightened his back.

'You're right,' he told her. 'I'll give up Josephine. I'll forget her. I'll forget everything, my whole robber's life. I'll go in for sheep. That's where peace is, in sheep-keeping. True or not, Mother? Could you do with another herdsman, sir?'

Old Farandol, great-grandson of a French major, straightened up proudly, just as Hopsika had done.

'Certainly, sir,' he said formally. 'Gladly. My sheep are threatened.'

'Wolves?' asked Hopsika eagerly.

'No,' said Farandol. 'Ghosts.'

He told Hopsika about the ruin, the moaning

wind, the red glow, the swirling mists and the lost Mary.

'And Corrie,' said Berto.

'And Maud,' said Berti.

'Maud is still there,' said Farandol. 'It's Bella who——'

But next morning it turned out that, without knowing it, Berti had spoken the truth after all. For Maud had vanished that night, without trace.

'And she had such beautiful little curls,' mourned Berta.

Hopsika drew his sword. 'I shall attack the ghosts tonight!' he cried. 'I'll force my way into the ruins and cut them apart!'

All well and good, but can you do that with ghosts?

21 Treasure Hunters

Berto's and Berti's eyes glowed at Hopsika's plan. What courage—right on the very doorstep!

But old Farandol shook his head. 'Cut them apart?' he said. 'Smoke and mist and wraiths? It would be easier to fight a dragon. At least it's solid.'

'Right,' said Hopsika, 'but ghosts are something new. That's what I find fun.'

Fun! Berto and Berti could scarcely breathe, it

was all so magnificent.

At lunchtime they ate green beans, and in the evening they ate green beans and bacon, because Berta approved of Hopsika's plan.

'All that whining over the girl Josephine,' she said. 'So sweet, so sweet, pah! He'll be better off dealing with ghosts. At least that's useful.'

The night was black as a mole tunnel. Even the silver spurs of Hopsika's boots found not a glimmer of light to reflect and, as the robber approached the ruins, the wind began to moan through the gaping windows.

'*Whoo-oo-oo!*' Hopsika moaned back. 'Come and show yourselves, if you dare!'

The wind blew chill in his face, and suddenly a reddish glow blazed up behind the walls, fear-somely illuminating the wobbly tower, and a gust of smoke swirled through the open gateway.

'Ah,' said Hopsika. 'The party lights are going on. That's nice.'

Drawing his sword, he advanced and began hacking at the smoke.

'*Atchoo!*'

He pulled out his red robber's handkerchief, held it to his nose and stepped through the gate.

'Cooee!' his voice echoed round the dilapidated building. 'Can I speak to the chief spook?'

A terrifying roar answered him from some-where in the depths.

'Are you in the dungeons?' called Hopsika.

No answer.

Swishing and swinging his sword, the robber groped his way on through the mist. 'Are you spook or smoke?' he cried. 'Speak up! Ow!' He sliced away once more. Bull's-eye! But it was a stone from the wall, which rolled away, rumbling, bump-bump-thud down the stairs.

'*Ow, ow, ow!*'

That came from the dungeon.

'Oh, excuse me,' cried Hopsika. 'Are you there, ghost? I've come to get the sheep back. Little Mary and Corrie and What's-her-name.'

Step by step he found his way to the dungeon stairs and descended, his silver spurs flashing in the ruddy glow.

'You really ought to have the stairs levelled up a bit, you know,' said Hopsika. 'They're dangerous. A human being could break his neck here.'

He groped onwards, but on the bottom-most step he suddenly felt two rigid ghostly hands clasped round his neck.

'Nice to meet you,' said the robber hoarsely. '*Ogh-ogh-ogh*, a breathtaking surprise.'

Two more ghostly hands gripped his waist and his booted legs were picked up too, and so they dragged him into a gloomy passageway.

'What an honour,' choked Hopsika, 'to be able to float between you like a ghost.'

But they said nothing. They laid him in a dark corner, tied his hands behind his back with thick rope, bound his legs tightly together and left him horribly alone.

A strange sort of civility, Hopsika thought to himself. And it's so dark here! I really wanted to see the ghosts. Come on, the old trick again.

He bent his legs up behind him, cut the rope

from his wrists with one stroke of his silver spurs, untied his feet and began the return journey, on hands and knees, mousy quiet.

The reddish light in the distance showed him the way, past the passageway and the stairs, to where the dungeons widened into a great vault. In the middle a fire was burning and, because there was no smoke so close to the ground, Hopsika could see something at last.

What he saw made his robber's eyes glitter.

Round the fire sat three men. Not ghosts, but skulking fellows, busy counting on scrabbling fingers; gold coins, silver chains, copper pots, diamond rings, rubies, pearls and a crystal goblet.

'Don't drop it,' hissed one of them.

Then Hopsika saw a deep hole in the floor and shovels beside it. He could see they were treasure-hunters.

22 The Poor Sheep

Hopsika could see it all. The three skulking fellows round the fire in the dungeons of the ruin were busy digging up the age-old treasure of a robber baron. Of course, they didn't want to be disturbed at it and in order to scare away curious nosy-parkers, they played at ghosts. And in order to have something to eat they kept on snatching one of old Farandol's sheep. The gnawed bones were lying in a corner, Hopsika saw, and a fine curly fleece, too. Bah, what brutes!

The robber stayed on his hands and knees for a moment, deep in thought, just like a grazing sheep.

'No,' he murmured. 'Politeness won't get me anywhere with fellows like these. It's better to beat them at their own game—that will make a nice change.'

He crawled silently towards the bone corner in a wide arc and picked up the fleece, while the three skulkers round the fire went on caressing and counting the gold and silver treasure with their fiddling fingers. One of the three was still holding a crystal goblet in his hand; he tapped it with his nail and raised the singing rim to his lips as if he were drinking wine from it.

'If you drop that, I'll——'

Meee-eh! they heard suddenly. It came from the dark corner full of bones. A hollow, terrifying bleat, and in the flickering light of the flames appeared a life-sized ghost-sheep. 'Vengeance!' it bleated, with weaving head. 'The ghost of Little Mary cries for vengeance. . . .'

With a loud crash and tinkle of splinters the crystal goblet fell on the stone floor, and the three blackguards crumpled to the ground with hoarse screams of terror.

The ghost-sheep came slowly nearer.

Baaa! it bleated once again and there was a sword sticking out from under its fleece, which can only happen with ghost-sheep. But the three did not see it, they only felt the sword pricking their

behinds. They leaped up with a screech, not daring to look round, rushed to the stairs, stumbled up them and raced out of the gates of the ruin. Away, away, far away from the horror down below. They looked like ghostly black birds, fleeing through the dark mountains, and the waggling tower of the ruin pointed after them like an evil finger.

But down below, Hopsika the sheep sat gazing gloomily into the fire.

'Poor Little Mary,' he murmured. 'Poor Corrie, poor What's-her-name.'

He gathered up the gold and silver and copper and diamonds and the fine treasures, placed them in Little Mary's skin, knotted it together and stood up painfully. With a gloomy sigh he swung the load over this shoulders and stumbled upwards, tripping over the worn treads. A human being could break his neck on them.

In the shepherd's hut no one had gone to bed.

Wide awake and tense with anxiety, they had been sitting round the table, turning the hour-glass from time to time. For the eighteenth time (Berto counted) for the nineteenth time (Berti counted), but through it all Berta sat counting her green beans, far into the hundreds.

'Not back yet,' sighed old Farandol. 'They have bedoozled him and bedonced him in the ruddy glow.' He certainly knew a bit of ghost language.

Then came the heavy tread of Hopsika's boots and the door was slowly opened.

'He's alive!' cried Berta, who was the first to see him, and her bowl of beans clattered to the floor.

Gaiety and dancing.

But the robber silently laid the knotted sheepskin on the table.

'Little Mary,' he said briefly.

Weeping and wailing.

Till Berta, her eyes flaming, croaked: 'It's Maud! I recognize the curls. Little Mary was moth-eaten.'

'Oh,' said Hopsika as solemnly as possible.

Then he unknotted Maud's skin and the sparsely lighted hut began to shine brightly with the splendour of all that gold and silver and copper and precious stones of the robber baron's treasure.

'*Aaah!*'

'Oh, a poor recompense for the irreplaceable

loss,' said the robber, respectfully removing his hat.

But the splendour was transferring itself to the eyes of the shepherd folk.

'By heaven, what entrails!' exclaimed Berta huskily.

'Rich, rich, rich!' cried Berto.

'At least a thousand new sheep!' cried Berti.

But old Farandol shook his head, the tears came into his eyes and—a loud, insistent banging on the door turned them all to stone.

23 Accident on the Road

Atsabootsa! The fun-town with its twelve fairgrounds and five circuses—the town took its toll of all its guests, even Irongrip, however strong the fat man was, with his daggers and pistols, even Irongrip was spinning after eighty-four turns on the roundabouts like a dog chasing its own tail. With lovely Josephine sobbing at his side.

'Away!' thundered Irongrip. 'We'll go away from here,' and they spun into the carriage—at last, something that went straight—out of the town, away from all the dizziness, away from Atsabootsa, the fun-town, bah! The horse felt no reins, it knew no other way than the way back, and began the laborious climb into the mountains because that was the direction they had come from.

It was really no more than a path, full of pot-holes and broken stones, winding its way up, but here and there down as well, because that's the way it goes in the mountains.

A coachman has to watch out on a path like that and use the brakes in time, because on the steep down-hill stretches the wagon picks up too much speed, more than the horse, and that's when you get a jack-knife. Look, it's happening already.

Irongrip is too dizzy for the reins and too dizzy for the brakes. He lets the horse go, and the carriage too. Cloppety-clop go the hooves and rumbledy-dumble go the wheels, fastest of all. The horse is not pulling, it is being pushed, but the carriage wants to go faster still, because this is a very steep stretch indeed.

Move, horse!

But the horse is attached to the carriage, so that has to move as well—the front wheels, that is. Not the back wheels, which go straight on, but the front wheels, which turn, horse and all, through ninety degrees, and then another ninety degrees, like an open knife which you snap shut. Only it makes a different sound, something like *grsjkrx*, with some horse-neighing and Iron curses, and sometimes everything falls over as well and rattles like a pile of twisted rods to the bottom of the slope.

But this breakdown went differently. Not only did the front wheels turn over, they broke off, like matchsticks. The back wheels shot sideways in a squealing skid and flew off the axle, so that the carriage continued its downward flight alone on its springs, like a sledge, but back to front. The unfortunate horse was still attached and had to gallop with it, also backwards.

Luckily it was only a short way.

Irongrip, accustomed to roundabouts, was still sitting on the box. Beautiful Josephine, paler than ever, was padded among the cushions on the back seat and asked in surprise why there was such a screeching.

'Hold your tongue,' Irongrip told her.

He jumped heavily to the ground so that his belts chinked and stooped to assess the damage.

'One wheel gone,' he muttered. 'Two wheels, three, and another. Four altogether.'

He straightened awkwardly. 'Numbskull!' he cursed at his horse, and the poor creature was far too nervous to reply. It stood quivering on its four legs. Luckily *they* were still all there.

'What now?' thundered Irongrip.

And the encircling mountains answered with their echo: 'Ow—ow—ow. . . .'

'Get help,' cried Josephine through the door. She had half opened it, perhaps in order to escape, but the horrid knight slammed it shut and dropped the bars round it so that the poor girl was back in her cage.

'You just wait here quietly!' he shouted to her, 'while I drum up a smith and a wheelwright. By thunder!'

He began to climb the slope on his iron feet, but in the desolate mountains, by thunder, there are no smiths and no wheelwrights either, at most a shepherd's hut, if you look long enough.

And Irongrip looked long. Huffing and puffing in his belly-belts, up hill, down dale, tripping over stones and cursing over gullies, until at last, long after midnight, he found a little hut from which a friendly light shone.

'Aha! At least there are people there.'

He stumbled to the door and banged on it with an iron fist.

There was a scraping inside and muffled voices and the chink of gold, as if it were being gathered up quickly. Finally an old, creaking voice called: 'We don't believe in ghosts any more. Just you go back to your ruins!'

'What?' thundered the fat man. 'Ghosts? I am Irongrip. And I've had an accident with my carriage. Open the door!'

Inside he seemed to hear a heavy sigh, a stifled cry which sounded a little like *Josephine*. But that must have been his imagination. There was more muttering and whispering and scraping, until at last the door was slowly opened. Irongrip blinked his eyes.

24 The Strength of Irongrip

The full light of a lamp was shining in Irongrip's face. Behind it he could see the vague figure of a shepherd with a hat, a long coat and a staff.

'*Whoops*,' said the shepherd. 'A whopping great knight at the door. Have you come to beg?'

'Beg?' thundered Irongrip. He opened his coat and let his belts with their thirteen daggers and pistols glitter in the light. 'I demand help, or I fire.' He was already holding two pistols.

The shepherd yawned loudly. 'In the middle of the night, too,' he said. 'My poor sheep would be woken up.'

'At once,' hissed Irongrip.

'Oh, do come in first. That will muffle the sound a little.'

Irongrip saw red, and stepped into the hut.

At the table sat a woman, behind a heap of green beans which she was topping and tailing and stringing. 'This is Berta,' said the shepherd, 'and these boys are Berti and Berto, oh, the other way round Berto and Berti. And there (he pointed to the bed) lies our poor sick father Farandol.'

'Useless!' shouted Irongrip. 'Just the boys, I can use them. Come at once!'

Berta looked up. 'Oh,' she said, 'they're nice and sharp.' She pointed to Irongrip's daggers. 'Let's have one of those for my beans.'

Irongrip exploded. 'My carriage!' he roared. 'My carriage has no wheels. All four have come off and——'

'Four?' said the shepherd. 'Is that all? You should have said so at once. Come on, boys, we'll fix them on again.'

He drew Berto and Berti outside with him, with Irongrip following like a great bewildered question mark. That voice, he thought hazily, that shepherd's voice, I've heard it somewhere . . . but he couldn't place him and he couldn't see that under his long coat the shepherd was wearing a pair of boots with silver spurs.

How indeed could Irongrip have expected to find his arch-enemy Hopsika in a shepherd's hut?

But on the other hand, Hopsika too, when he heard the name Irongrip shouted out with that knock at the door, had turned first pale and then red with amazement. 'Josephine,' he stammered, and suddenly saw his chance. Quick, quick, away with the treasure, on with Farandol's clothes, into bed with the old man in his underclothes and open the door.

'Is it much further?' Hopsika asked and he began to whistle a merry tune.

The carriage was still standing on its springs, the bars were still round it, the horse was neighing sorrowfully and Josephine was asleep on the soft back seat.

'A nice cage,' said Hopsika. 'Do you keep canaries?'

'The wheels!' barked Irongrip. 'Look for the wheels.'

Berto and Berti, with a lantern each, began to peer between rocks, down crevices and under bushes. They found one. They found another one. The third was hanging in a tree. The fourth remained unfound, however much they called.

'Won't three do?' asked Hopsika. 'You yourself could act as the fourth wheel. You're strong enough.'

Irongrip yelped. 'Put them on!' he commanded. He unlocked the wall of bars with the rusty key, snapped it back onto the roof of the carriage and tipped the whole vehicle up. Berto and Berti each banged on one back wheel. 'Done!'

'Now the front,' cried Hopsika gaily. 'Ah, Sir Knight, unharness your horse, it will be easier.'

Irongrip did so.

'And now you'll have to play horses,' said Hopsika still more gaily. 'Between the shafts. It's easier to lift there.'

Irongrip did so.

'One two . . .' cried Hopsika.

Berto banged on the left front wheel, and suddenly Hopsika cried: 'Hey there, look, the fourth wheel! There it is, under your carriage. No, no, you just stay there and lift. Higher, still higher.'

Berti was tugging at the newly found wheel, but Hopsika was up to something else—his clever little plan.

With a thick rope he bound Irongrip's hands to the shafts at lightning speed as the strong man lifted. Firm as a rock he bound them. And to the furious roar the robber answered only: 'Well, horsie, my little horsie friend on two legs, would you like to pull, with your iron muscles?'

And in the dawning light of day he threw off his shepherd's dress and showed himself in his true robber form.

'Hopsika!' yelled Irongrip, jerking at his ropes. At last the wily knight had recognized his arch-enemy.

'Whoa horse, whoa,' said the robber. 'Not so fast.'

He took a moving leave of Berto and Berti. 'Tell old Farandol that he may keep the treasure from the ruins. And be kind enough to hang my mother's portrait on the saddle of my horse and send it after me.'

Then he opened the door of the coach.

'Josephine,' stammered the robber. 'At last, at last! I'm taking you back to your father.'

'Hopsika,' she answered, 'I want to stay with you. Shall we get married?'

'Oh, fine,' said Hopsika.

But first Irongrip had to haul the two of them home like a horse in the shafts. It was a long way.

'Forward!' cried Hopsika, cracking his whip.

25 A Difficult Return

That day travellers saw a strange procession riding up the steep path through the mountains. First came a loose horse, then a fat, sweating man pulling a coach and after that another loose horse with a picture dangling from its saddle. The first horse and the last whinnied angrily at one another.

On the box of the coach sat a thin young man with long legs like sticks. He was whistling a merry tune, but from time to time he called to the horses: 'Stop that bad language!'

In the coach sat a girl with dark eyes like still pools.

'And I have my love
And I have my love
Sweet Josephine is mine!

And I need no more
And I need no more
I need no more repine!'

sang the young man on the box.

Some of the travellers shook their heads sympathetically; others laughed, but those who are reading this will have to follow the procession further to find out what happened next.

'Forward!' Hopsika cried again. 'At the gallop!' He cracked the whip—in the air, of course.

Now Irongrip really was strong, but after about an hour of running up hill and down dale he was beginning to lose his breath.

'Whoa then,' cried the robber. 'Hup, hup, whoa! We're just going to stop and have a bite to eat.'

That sounded nice, but in this inhospitable spot

there was not much edible food to be found.

'My tummy's rumbling!' puffed Irongrip.

'Yes, yes, in a minute,' said Hopsika. 'When we pass an oat field.'

He unhooked the painting from the horse and went to sit beside Josephine on the back seat with it. 'My mother,' said the robber tenderly. 'Beautiful, eh?'

'She looks so stern,' said Josephine.

'What did you say, stern?'

'I think so, yes.'

'Mother!' cried Hopsika, 'I'm not doing anything, am I? I'm not robbing, I'm not stealing, I gave the treasure to the shepherds, I've saved Josephine, I've—'

'She's still looking stern,' said Josephine.

Irongrip was beginning to snort again.

'Hungry! Let me loose!'

'Could that be it?' asked Josephine. 'Our carriage horse?'

'Never!' cried Hopsika. 'No, Mother, no, I won't do it. I won't let him go. He's earned his punishment.'

He put the portrait down crossly between the seats, gave Josephine a kiss, jumped onto the box again and cracked the whip angrily. 'Forward. At the gallop!'

Irongrip surged forward again, up hill and down dale, with Hopsika stubborn and silent on the box. They rode on like this all afternoon, until at last, towards evening, a house came in sight, lonely among the hills.

'Ah!' cried Hopsika, pulling on the reins. 'Stop.

That's enough.'

First he helped Josephine down with the portrait, then he went to Irongrip, took the belts with the thirteen daggers and thirteen pistols from his tummy and flung them away among the nettles, untied Irongrip from the shafts, harnessed his own horse to them, pushed the fat man into the coach and slapped the horse with the flat of his hand so that the beast clattered off at a startled gallop, the coach with its furiously roaring occupant swaying behind it.

'There they go. Hurrah! What a relief. He's gone. Listen to the birds. Glad, glad, glad!' Hopsika danced around, he danced around with Josephine, he sang, he whistled, he hopped.

'Come on, Josephine, let's have something nice to eat here first,' he cried merrily.

'Oh?' said Josephine. 'Who lives here, then?'

'No idea,' said Hopsika. 'At any rate it's someone who eats. So we'll simply eat with him.'

'Simply?' asked Josephine.

'Yes, with a knife and fork,' said Hopsika, 'and a respectable table napkin. You can do that, can't you?'

'Yes, but . . .' Josephine began hesitantly.

'I don't know anything about yes but,' cried Hopsika. 'Isn't that right Mother?' He put the portrait under one arm, took Josephine with the other and walked to the front door. 'These people will be glad that someone has turned up at last. Just you see.'

Hopsika pressed the bell firmly. He was quite his old cheerful self again.

Ting-a-ling! The bell echoed in the hallway, and at once a deafening screeching and fluttering and chirping and whistling broke out.

'One thing's sure,' said the robber, 'a bird-lover lives here.'

Shuffling footsteps could be heard, the door opened hesitantly and there stood—in big slippers, with a big nose and big spectacles—a mean little man.

'Hallo, Uncle!' cried Hopsika merrily. 'Here we are at last.'

He took his hat off ceremoniously. 'Been a long time, eh?'

The mean little man stared at the robber through his glasses and pulled strange faces. Then in a shrill canary-voice he uttered:

'Pee-eet?'

'That's it, Pete! I knew you would recognize me right away. And this is Josephine.'

26 Uncle

Hopsika drew Josephine inside. A sickly gust of bird-scented air came to meet them.

'Hmm,' he said to the mean little man, 'I can tell you've already got a delicious chicken on the stove for us.'

He should not have said that, because the mean

little fellow almost attacked him with rage. 'Stove?' he rasped. 'Stove? I don't put my sweethearts on the stove!'

'Oh no, no, of course not,' soothed Hopsika, 'I don't either, you know,' and he put a tender arm around Josephine. 'I was confusing it with pea soup. How's business, Uncle?'

'Business?' the little man grated still more angrily. 'I don't do business.'

'Oh no, no, of course not! Why did I say business?' Hopsika laughed loudly. 'You do birds, I mean——'

'Ornithology!' snarled the little man. It sounded like a curse, and his pointed chin stuck out threateningly.

'Pardon, Uncle——?' said Hopsika.

'Or-ni-thol-o-gist!'

'Ah! Uncle Ornithologist, of course, of course!' Hopsika beamed with recognition. 'How could I forget your name like that, Uncle Orni——'

'Name, name, name?' the mean little man was screeching loud enough for ten. 'It's my *profession.* I study jays and jackdaws, warblers and wagtails, parrots and peewits.'

'I understand,' said Hopsika, 'the birds and the bee——'

'NO! No insects!'

'——eaters I mean. Bee-eaters,' Hopsika amended hastily.

'Ah . . .' all the anger disappeared from the little man as if by magic and he cocked his head like a robin. 'Bee-eaters, aha . . . I haven't any. Good idea!'

He spun round and hopped down the long passage and into a room.

Hopsika and Josephine followed. The room was full of cages and the cages were full of the fluttering and whistling of birds.

'What little darlings!' cried Josephine.

'Yes, nice,' said Hopsika. 'What do you do with them, Uncle?'

'Let them out!' cried the little man.

'Interesting,' said the robber. 'You catch birds in order to let them go?'

'Right. And then I rise into the air with them and study their flight.'

'Ah!' cried Hopsika brightly. 'You fly yourself. How—er——'

But a cry from Josephine interrupted him.

'Ow!' she cried. 'Beast!'

The little man spun round wrathfully. 'My macaw!' he screeched, 'keep away from it, miss. No fingers in the cage, own fault. Yes, yes, it's bleeding!'

'The creature is hungry,' said Hopsika, laying a comforting arm round Josephine. 'We are too, Uncle. You were expecting us, weren't you?'

'Oh yes,' said the little man. 'There's birdseed in the kitchen.'

Hopsika's head began to spin, but Josephine made straight for the kitchen where she opened every tin and set to with pots and pans.

They made a strange meal of sweet corn, lettuce, oats, barley and prunes.

'It's good, Uncle,' said Hopsika with his mouth full.

'Bee-eaters,' trilled the little man. 'Tomorrow I must get some——' Suddenly he stared into Hopsika's eyes through his spectacles. 'Uncle,' he said. 'Whose uncle am I, actually?'

The robber swallowed. 'Mine,' he said.

'Oh?' the eyes behind the glasses became hazy. 'Do you mean the great-grandson of my great-aunt on my mother's side?'

'Exactly!' cried Hopsika.

'Oh. You're a postman, then?'

Hopsika swallowed more painfully. 'Well, not exactly that, Uncle.'

'Oh no? What are you, then?'

'A ro—er . . . rockinghorse-maker,' said the robber quickly.

'Heee . . .' once again he cocked his head like a robin. 'Niece Emily was writing to me only the other day about her Dirk with all his express-letters—you are Dirk, aren't you?'

Hopsika turned red. 'Er, did you say Dirk? Am I Dirk? Er . . . No, I'm Pete, aren't I? Pee-eet, I mean . . .'

Never before in this story had the robber Hopsika been so embarrassed. Josephine looked pale and bit her fingers even harder than the macaw had done.

'Now then, who?' asked the mean little man, his eyes boring into Hopsika's.

But that was not the worst thing. Still worse was the loud banging which suddenly broke the icy silence. Banging on the front door. The birds screeched in their cages, Josephine began to tremble and Hopsika realized who it was.

'Hee,' crowed the little man. 'More post, eh?'

He was about to get up, but Hopsika was ahead of him. 'Don't trouble yourself, Uncle,' said the robber, running towards the front door. 'I'll get it.'

He peered through the letter-box.

'Didn't I say so?' he muttered.

Outside, in the pale evening light, stood Irongrip.

27 The Siege

But Irongrip was not alone. The nasty fat fellow had collected thirteen farm lads, who were flourishing thirteen hayforks menacingly.

'The house is surrounded, Hopsika,' he cried. 'Come out, if you dare.'

'Of course!' Hopsika called back through the letter-box. 'The second turning on the right and then keep left. You can't miss it.' And without waiting for an answer he returned, whistling, to the kitchen, where the mean little man looked at him enquiringly: 'No post?'

'Oh no,' said Hopsika airily, 'it wasn't the postman, it was a poor traveller who had lost his way.'

Josephine looked questioningly at him and Hopsika gave her a wink. 'Good as gold,' he said, 'polite and modest and——'

A furious threatening banging sounded again on the front door.

'Dearie me, perhaps the poor traveller is hungry,' said the little man, jumping up. 'I'll just go and let him in.'

'Of course, Uncle,' cried Hopsika. 'That's truly generous. But you sit there and let me do it.'

He ran quickly back to the passage, opened the flap of the letter-box and asked loudly, 'Would you like a little bowl of soup, sir?'

'I'll stick you on my pitchfork,' thundered Irongrip outside.

'Just a second,' said the robber.

He hurried back to the kitchen. 'He'd like some soup,' he announced, 'and a cob of corn as well. But our traveller is too modest to come in. I'll take it to him myself.'

'Dearie me,' said the mean little fellow once again.

'Can I help?' asked Josephine, trembling.

'There, there,' said Hopsika, and back he went to the front door again with the soup and the corn-cob.

'It isn't very much,' he called through the letter-box, 'but it comes from a good heart.'

Irongrip leaned forward. 'You'll not get out of this alive, Hopsika,' he roared, but at the *ka* of Hopsika a fat cob of corn was stuffed into his mouth and a splash of soup to go with it.

'*Gblurbb!*' cursed the fat man, spitting. 'I'll get you, Hopsika. I'll stay here with my thirteen men for as long as it takes. I'll starve you out.'

Hopsika dropped the flap of the letter-box and

skipped back to the kitchen. 'A grateful man,' he said, touched.

'A bit noisy,' said Uncle.

'Yes, he wanted you to hear,' said Hopsika.

'Naturally,' said Josephine, her voice quivering. 'It sounded very touching. Has he gone now?'

'Well,' said Hopsika, 'he's just eating it all up. And then. . . .'

Yes, what then?

They could go on staying with Uncle, the robber fixed that up easily, and Irongrip stayed outside. But there was not much question of sleep that night. Whenever Hopsika peeped out through a gap in the curtains he could see the pitchforks shining in the light of the moon and stars.

'Well polished,' he murmured.

But Josephine had no eyes for that. 'We're trapped, Hopsika,' she whispered. 'You should never have let him go.'

'I did it for Mother,' said the robber.

Josephine looked at him with her dark eyes. 'That's wonderful of you,' she said sweetly.

Then came the practical question: 'What shall we do tomorrow?'

Hopsika tried to think out a plan, but it was Uncle himself who turned up with a plan next morning. He appeared quite early, rubbing his hands alertly, oddly dressed in knee-breeches, with woollen stockings, a check jacket and sports cap.

'Up!' he crowed. 'Up and away, up on the hunt for bee-eaters.'

'But, Uncle,' cried Hopsika, 'shouldn't you—'

'No shirking! Come along with you, lend a

hand.' Uncle got a big basket filled with ropes and rags, looking like a badly folded tent, and dragged the thing to the front door.

'Uncle, I would . . .' cried Hopsika again, but it was too late. The little man opened the door briskly and there stood Irongrip, broad and fat and threatening, with thirteen pitchforks behind him.

'Got you!' he roared.

But he was wrong, because Hopsika's agile form dived through the arm and slammed the door shut again.

'Wretched robber!' shouted Irongrip.

It was very audible.

Uncle stiffened. He turned to Hopsika with flashing eyes: 'Robber?' he exclaimed. 'You're not a postman, you're not a great-great-nephew, you're not Pete, you're a *robber*?'

'Oh, Uncle . . .' Hopsika began.

'Out!' shouted the little man, red with rage and tripping over the full basket.

'Think of your tent,' said Hopsika.

Apparently this was worse still. Uncle turned white-hot. 'Tent?' he shouted, 'tent? Do you think I study my birds from a *tent*? Ha, I do it from the air, sir. In full flight.'

And pointing to the basket of ropes and rags he cried: 'That, Mr Robber, is my *balloon*.'

28 The Weight of Mother

The mean little man was still pointing proudly to his balloon when Irongrip began roaring again from outside.

'Open the door!' they heard. 'I'll stick you on thirteen pitchforks at once, Hopsika. And I demand Josephine back.'

'Oh, what a nasty man he is,' sobbed Josephine.

'Deceiver!' the little man hissed at Hopsika. 'Nephew, indeed, when you were a robber all the time! Be off with you!'

Hopsika was certainly caught between two very hot fires: but then an affectionate smile broke out on his face. He beamed with contentment and said brightly: 'That's it, dear Uncle, that's just what we'll do: be off.'

Uncle's mouth fell open.

'To catch bee-eaters,' Hopsika added. 'Got a net?' He began to drag the basket along the passage to the stairs.

'Hee, hee!' cried the little man.

'How can we get up to the roof?' asked Hopsika.

'Impudence! Out *there* I said!'

'I'm going,' said Hopsika. 'Where's the gas-pipe?'

Josephine saw his plan at once. 'Right!' she cried. 'Up to the bee-eaters!' She rushed forward to help Hopsika.

'I'm going to open the door,' threatened the little man.

'I wouldn't do that, Uncle,' said Hopsika. 'There'd be such a lot of mess with all those men and pitchforks. I asked for the gas-pipe.'

While the little man went on hopping to and fro in a rage, doing nothing to help, Hopsika and Josephine pulled the basket with the balloon in it to the attic, and from there through a trapdoor onto the roof.

'A gentle breeze,' said the robber, sniffing the wind.

Irongrip was still thundering at the door.

Josephine found a long gas-pipe in the kitchen, and unrolled it up to the roof.

'What, what, what?' shouted Uncle, 'this won't do at all!'

'The bee-eaters are chirping,' said Hopsika, coming down the stairs. 'Get your net and come with us.' He turned the gas tap and, with a gentle hiss, the gas ran up the pipe to the ropes and rags on the roof, to blow them up into a balloon.

'I'm going to break down the door!' Irongrip roared threateningly.

'The man has no patience,' Hopsika remarked. 'Just a moment!' he called to Irongrip. 'I'll be out at once!'

He took Uncle soothingly by the hand. 'Don't get so excited,' he said kindly. 'The fat fellow isn't too bad. He slanders me a bit, but you musn't take any notice of him. Come on, the sky is blue and the bee——'

'Hopsika!' yelled Josephine. 'Turn off the tap. It's full!'

A tremendous blow cracked the front door and the two gleaming prongs of a pitchfork stuck menacingly through.

Hopsika turned off the tap. 'Shall we go, then?' he said, pulling Uncle up behind him. 'How many were you thinking of? Six or seven of the jolly little fellows? Shall we be able to catch that many?'

Like wax in his hands, the mean little man followed Hopsika onto the roof, where the balloon was dancing merrily in the wind.

'Oh, what a beauty!' cried the robber. 'What a colour, what breadth, what grace. It's well tied down, I hope?'

Josephine had tied the anchor rope to the chimney and put a number of roof tiles in the basket for ballast.

'Good work,' said Hopsika, 'you're the right wife for me.'

Josephine blushed. She wanted to fly into Hopsika's arms, but a fresh roar from the garden made them look over the parapet. Irongrip and his henchmen had discovered the balloon.

'Listen to the people cheering us,' said Hopsika. 'A take-off like this is a great event for them. Get into the basket, Uncle.'

Uncle was already in it, for the cracking of the front door had redoubled now that the besiegers were set on preventing the escape by air.

Hopsika stepped into the basket as well, and he

was just lifting his left leg to cut the rope with his razor-sharp spur when Josephine said: 'Mother!'

'Ah!' cried the robber, slapping himself on the forehead. 'Josephine, you guardian angel.'

He got out of the basket again. 'Just a moment, Uncle,' he said calmly and climbed down again through the trapdoor to get the portrait.

At that moment the front door splintered open and a howling mob came stamping into the passage. But Hopsika was quick. With his mother under his arm he reappeared on the roof, while those below were still tramping up the stairs.

'Now we're off at last,' he said, hacking with his heel. But the rope fell limply. Nothing happened.

'Ballast out!' ordered the robber.

One roof tile, two roof tiles, three, four. Even Uncle helped. The attic stairs were groaning under the tramping feet and the rabble was coming unpleasantly close.

'One more,' cried Hopsika, 'then we're off.'

Irongrip stuck his head through the trapdoor.

'Catch!' cried Hopsika, throwing the last roof tile at the fat man.

It gave them a moment's respite. Just enough for the balloon to rise a few centimetres, laboriously clear the parapet and hover over the garden. But it did not rise.

Mother's portrait was too heavy.

29 Up to the Bee-eaters

'I'll get you!' roared Irongrip, leaning dangerously over the gutter and shaking his fist until he almost lost his balance. 'Just you wait!'

With his thirteen men the fat man pelted down through the house and appeared on the lawn

'He's got a plan,' said Josephine, peering over the edge of the basket.

'There are no plans in that fat head,' said Hopsika. 'Hey!' he called down, 'remember the daisies! You're treading them in!' Meanwhile the mean little man was flailing madly about with his net.

'Higher,' he piped, 'we must go higher. There are no bee-eaters here.'

'Up!' cried Josephine as well. 'Quick, Hopsika, quick!'

She was not talking about bee-eaters, she was looking at Irongrip. Clearly pursuing a plan, the fat man was groping among the stinging nettles further off.

'That's where you threw his pistols,' Josephine called to Hopsika. 'He's looking for them to shoot the balloon down.'

'Ow!' roared Irongrip, for the nettles were stinging painfully.

But the thirteen men began to beat down the weeds with their pitchforks. It would not be long before——

'There's one!' piped Uncle, pointing high up in the air. 'I can hear it cheeping!'

It was clear that the three balloonists would have to rise a good bit higher—the basket was too heavy, something had to go.

'Ballast!' cried the mean little man.

But there was no more ballast on board.

'The portrait!' piped Uncle.

Hopsika paled. 'Never,' he said, clutching Mother.

'Your bird-net,' cried Josephine.

Uncle paled. 'Never,' he said, clutching his net.

'Aha!' roared Irongrip, 'got them. Ouch!'

There was not much time left.

'Hopsika, your boots,' yelled Josephine, trying to pull off her own shoes and throw them overboard, but the robber did not want that. 'Keep them on, sweetheart. They're much too pretty for that fatty below. He's going to get something else.'

The fatty below drew himself up to his full height, the belt with the thirteen pistols in his hand. He selected one with care.

'Oh, Uncle,' said Hopsika, pointing upwards, 'there's a rope crooked up there. Just climb up into the rigging, experienced balloonist as you are!'

The mean little man looked up. 'I can't see anything,' he said.

'Can't you climb?' said Hopsika.

Uncle was quite willing to show him. In a

twinkling he was shinning nimbly up the rope.

At the same time Hopsika was hanging Mother's portrait on a slip-knot, scooping Josephine under one arm and pulling himself up on the ropes with the other.

'Hoopla!' he cried, swinging both legs with their silver-flashing spurs in a circle.

Irongrip aimed two pistols at once. The balloon, big and bright, directly above his head, was a simple target.

'Ha, ha, Hopsika!' he shouted, 'come down nicely, now. *I'll* catch Josephine.'

But before he could shoot, something else came down.

The robber Hopsika had cut through all the ropes of the basket with his flailing spurs so that the heavy wicker object plummeted to the ground. Well-aimed, too, for the basket neatly caged Irongrip's fat form and nipped the salvo of shots in the bud.

At the same moment, having lost all that weight, the balloon rose with dizzying speed, to a dizzying height.

'Yes!' piped Uncle. 'Bee-eaters! We're going straight to them!' He reached for his net and looked down, bemused. 'Hey, what's happened to the basket?' he croaked, cocking his head.

'Oh,' said Hopsika, 'the thing was too heavy. Just ballast. We're quite comfortable sitting on the ring, aren't we?'

'Well, quite . . .'

Josephine clung to Hopsika, for the ground was a very long way below them.

'My net!' moaned Uncle.

'Oh,' said Hopsika, 'I'll catch them under my hat. Marvellous view, isn't it, Mother?'

The portrait turned in the wind, as if taking a good look round. And it was the wind which blew the balloon along, with the three air travellers.

Irongrip, prostrate among the stinging nettles, and his thirteen farm lads vanished out of sight, far below them.

But there was one thing which did not vanish. Running, speeding, racing, jumping over hedges and ditches, galloping up hill and down dale, it followed the onward gliding balloon. Hopsika could see it by the dust clouds. 'My horse,' he cried, 'my faithful horse!'

30 The Last Battle

From the balloon, wafted high in the blue sky by the wind, Hopsika watched with tears in his eyes as the faithful beast below kept up, over valleys and hills, over hedges and ditches.

How long could the horse keep it up?

Josephine asked: 'Are we going the right way, Hopsika? Is the wind blowing us home?'

And the mean little man cried: 'Look, look, the bee-eater sings as it flies. Its beak keeps time with its wings. Catch it, Hopsika!' But the robber turned the gas-tap so that the balloon crumpled up with a hiss and began to descend.

'I can't reach it like this!' piped the little man.

But the robber turned the gas-tap further still, until, hovering just over his horse, he could grasp its reins. 'Whoa!' he cried, 'stand still.'

The horse was steaming.

'Uncle,' said Hopsika, 'we're going to take our leave now. And to make up for the lost balloon basket, I've something else for you.'

He put the little man on the saddle of his horse and tied the dangling ropes of the balloon to it.

'I don't want a horse,' piped Uncle.

'You're not getting one,' said Hopsika. He lifted the portrait and Josephine to the ground and loosened the girths with a jerk.

The balloon, no longer weighed down by Josephine and Hopsika, shot into the air like an arrow, with Uncle perched like a horseman in the saddle.

'Farewell!' cried Hopsika, raising his hat with a flourish. 'Thank you again for all your help and trouble, and a good bag to you!'

As the wind veered the mean little man flew crowing homeward, gazing happily at all the bee-eaters he passed.

And, at a walking pace, with Josephine and the portrait in front of him on the horse's back, Hopsika took the homeward road, without a saddle. It was a long way. . . .

Later on, when the trampling of hooves and rattle of wheels approached them from behind, the old robber instinct awoke in Hopsika.

'Just a moment,' he said.

Getting up speed, he was about to make his old accustomed leap onto the lead-horse of the team, but the coachman had recognized the robber and reined in.

'Ah, that makes it easier this time,' cried Hopsika cheerfully. He dismounted, opened the door of the carriage, removed his hat politely and began: 'Gentlemen——'

But he was interrupted by a hoarse cry from one of the passengers.

'Come, come my dear sir,' said Hopsika soothingly. 'Have no fear. This time I'm not concerned with money but——'

A still louder cry, a sob and outstretched arms interrupted Hopsika once again.

'Well, well, an attack?' he cried in surprise. But the passenger leaped past the robber and out of the carriage, uttering a third cry which was at last understandable: 'Josephine!'

He pressed her to his heart.

And Josephine stammered: 'Father!'

Then Hopsika recognized the man who had promised him a thousand golden florins to steal back his daughter—how long ago now?

'And he succeeded, Father!' she cried, pointing to Hopsika.

'Oh yes,' said the robber, 'it just took a little longer than I thought.'

Josephine's father could not get a word out; with a lump in his throat and tears in his eyes he groped in his coat pocket and pulled out a heavy purse.

'Never mind that,' said Hopsika. 'I'd rather have her.'

Lump and tears disappeared in a flash. 'What's that?' asked the father sternly.

'Quite simple,' said Hopsika, 'I want to marry her.'

'You?' cried the man. 'A robber? Marry my daughter?'

'Yes!' cried Josephine. She let her father go and flung her arms round Hopsika.

'No question of it!' cried the man, feeling for his purse again.

At that moment there was more trampling of hooves and rattling of wheels from a distance. A second coach was approaching, at full speed, and even before the horse could come to a stop a heavy figure jumped from it.

Irongrip.

'What a coincidence!' Hopsika called to him. 'I've just returned Josephine to her father. You'll have to have it out with him.'

The poor father turned pale with fright. 'No,' he wailed, shuddering. 'No! Hopsika, help me!'

'Why should I do that?' asked the robber, as Irongrip approached with drawn dagger and pistol.

'Because,' screeched the man, 'because then you can marry Josephine.'

'Really?' asked Hopsika.

'Really!' the man cried desperately.

'Word of honour?' asked Hopsika.

Irongrip was very close.

'Word of honour,' screeched the father.

Then the robber Hopsika went into action. He danced like a whirlwind round the stout rogue, kicked all thirteen daggers and all thirteen pistols out of his fingers and out of his belts with his spindly shanks, and cried: 'Catch me if you can!' Then he jumped into the first carriage and out again on the other side, so that Irongrip, who had jumped after him, was stuck roaring between the seats, full length on the floor.

'There you are!' Hopsika slammed down the bars and ordered the coachman to drive straight to the police.

'That's it,' said the robber, brushing down his trousers, 'now let's get married at once, then I can go home and read a book in peace at last.'

And that was just what happened.

Mother's portrait was given the place of honour in the house, and whenever Hopsika had a book out he looked up at it, like a good boy. But when he looked into Josephine's dark, velvety eyes his robber's heart began to beat tumultuously.

That's life: adventure always calls.

THE DEMON BIKE RIDER

Robert Leeson

There was a ghost on Barker's Bonk: a horned demon that made a terrible howling noise as it glided along in the dusk – on a bicycle. When Mike and his friends first heard about the Demon Bike Rider they thought a bike-riding ghost could only be a joke. But then one night they saw it, and heard it, and suddenly they were running so fast there was no time to laugh.

Other odd things keep happening. A mysterious stranger seems to be making secret explorations of the old cottage on the Bonk. And who on earth planted a whole lot of trees upside down in Mr Whitehurst's garden? It is all to do with the Demon Bike Rider, whose story is finally unravelled with as much hilarity as haunting.

The King of the Copper Mountains

PAUL BIEGEL

For more than a thousand years King Mansolain has reigned over the Copper Mountains, but now he is old and tired. To keep his heart beating, he must hear exciting stories.

So one by one the animals of his Kingdom come to tell their tales – the fierce wolf, the chattering squirrel, and the three-headed dragon, breathing fire. The beetle sits close to the King's ear to tell his story while the other animals lie on his beard. Next comes the mighty lion and last of all, the dwarf. He prophesies that the old King *could* live a thousand more years, but only if the Wonder Doctor arrives in time . . .

The Little Captain is also a Lion.

For eight-year-olds and upwards.

Simon and the Witch

MARGARET STUART BARRY

Simon's friend the witch lives in a neat, semi-detached house with a television and a telephone, but she has never heard of Christmas or been to the seaside. However, she has a wand, which she loses, causing confusion at the local constabulary, and a mean-looking cat called George, who eats the furniture when she forgets to feed him. The witch shows Simon how to turn the school gardener into a frog, and she and her relations liven up a Hallowe'en party to the delight of the children and the alarm of the local dignitaries. With a witch for a friend, Simon discovers, life is never dull.

Very highly recommended by ILEA's *Contact* magazine: '. . . who could resist such a lively character?'

You will find more adventures of Simon and the Witch in *The Return of the Witch*, also a Lions paperback.

Funny Folk

AIDAN CHAMBERS

Not very far away and not that long ago there was an iron man who enjoyed light bulbs for a quick snack but preferred gramophone records for a more substantial meal . . . and an enterprising parson who pedalled so fast his bicycle ran away with him . . . and a very merry monk who left his dignity at the monastery to enjoy all the fun of the fair with some strange and hilarious consequences.

In this wonderfully funny collection Aidan Chambers, a well-known writer and critic, has selected and recounted some of his favourite comic tales, rhymes and jokes, both traditional and modern, and all guaranteed to make your toes curl with fun and delight.

'In County Durham, where I grew up, we have a saying: "There's nowt so funny as folk".' *Aidan Chambers*

'Full of meat, *Funny Folk* really is funny . . . a source book for the sort of jokes children really love.' *TLS*